VIOLENCE AMONG STUDENTS
AND SCHOOL STAFF

VIOLENCE AMONG STUDENTS AND SCHOOL STAFF

Understanding and Preventing the Causes of School Violence

DISCARD

Sean M. Brooks Ph.D.

Foreword by Mark Pearcy, Ph.D.

Edited by Holli Bryan
Cover design by Chris Berge
Foreword by Mark Pearcy, Ph.D.

ISBN: 1539803627
ISBN 13: 9781539803621
Library of Congress Control Number: 2016918276
CreateSpace Independent Publishing Platform
North Charleston, South Carolina

Printed in the United States of America
North Charleston, South Carolina

Disclaimer: At the time of this book's publication, all citations and URLs available are accurate and the most current available. The author and publisher are not responsible for any changing of information to websites or references, nor are we responsible for any changes that may exist in the future. Although the author and publisher have made every effort to ensure that the information in this book was correct at press time, the author and publisher do not assume and hereby disclaim any liability to any party for any loss, damage or disruption caused by errors or omissions, whether such errors or omissions result from negligence, accident or any other cause. This book should serve only as a general guide and not as the sole source of subject information. This book is intended only to educate and entertain. This book is not intended as a substitute for the medical advice of licensed physicians. The reader should regularly consult a physician in matters relating to his or her health and particularly with respect to any symptoms that may require diagnosis or medical attention.

Contents

Far more crucial than what we know or do not know is what we do not want to know.

We lie loudest when we lie to ourselves.

—Eric Hoffer

Foreword

For years I have worked with pre-service teachers at the university level. Prior to that, I was a high-school teacher in the public-school system for nineteen years. Before that, even before I graduated high school, I was part of an outburst of violence that typifies in many ways the worst of what educators can contemplate—as well as represents one of the last things we should ever worry about.

When I was a senior at Pinellas Park High School in Largo, Florida, on February 11, 1988, two students, sophomores Jason McCoy and Jason Harless, brought handguns to school. During lunch, administrators Nancy Blackwelder and Richard Allen confronted the boys. The situation escalated, and a student teacher named Joseph Bloznalis, who was observing the scene, tried to grab Harless. In the fight that ensued, Harless began to fire his weapon in a cafeteria jammed with students.

Within a few seconds, three people were shot. Bloznalis was shot in his leg. Blackwelder was shot three times in her abdomen and Richard Allen through the head. The boys ran. The police confronted them. Harless was shot in the shoulder and arrested. McCoy, who had never fired his gun, ran from the school and was arrested later. Bloznalis and Blackwelder both survived their wounds. Allen died in the hospital six days after the shooting (Leisner, 1988). The unreal nature of the event affected everyone connected with the school and the community. How could this happen here, at a typical suburban high school?

The attackers later claimed that they were only going to show the guns to their friends. They stated that they had stolen the guns because they were going to run away from home and that they wanted to protect themselves. The two students were arrested and jailed, and the faculty, staff, and student body mourned but eventually moved on. In fact, on the twentieth anniversary of the shooting in 2008, the school community chose not to observe the date in any formal manner. The principal at the time, John Johnston, said that the faculty members who had been at the school in 1988 didn't want to commemorate the event. He said, "They would prefer to have it go forward as a regular day" (Winchester, 2008).

Routinely when pre-service teachers ask me about the prospect of school violence, I tell them this story from my own experience. Then I follow it immediately with a fact that most pre-service educators have difficulty believing: schools are, by and large, overwhelmingly safe. Despite the high-profile nature of mass shootings over recent years at both elementary and secondary schools as well as within universities, gun violence has decreased steadily since the early 1990s (Booth, Van Hasselt, & Vecchi, 2011).

This fact does little, I've found, to soften my students' anxiety over the prospect of violence in their classrooms. The nature of their fears is even more alarming when we confront the fact that the issues of school violence, particularly incidents that are less high profile, are in fact very real. Studies that document the general decline in school-based homicides also chart the rise in aggravated assaults, drug and narcotic violations, weapons charges, violence toward school staff, and, most ubiquitously, bullying in all forms (Dinkes, et al., 2007; Noonan & Mara, 2007). Why then do student teachers have an outsized fear of an incident, which, though undeniably disturbing to contemplate, is so much less likely to occur than these types of incidents?

My suspicion is that much of the problem is derived from the natural human tendency to assume the worst in a situation. For example, the universally acknowledged safety of air travel does little to ease those who find the experience terrifying, largely by contemplating the most unlikely of events, the crash of an airliner. So, too, it seems with school violence. While concerned to the point of obsession with mass shootings and homicides, we have overlooked the very real instances of violence that are considerably more common in our schools.

As any effective educator would attest, the best antidote to misunderstanding is an accurate education on the relevant issues. Education on the subject of school-related violence is vital, not just with regard to horrifying yet rare incidents (like that at Pinellas Park High School in 1988) but also to the vicious and more commonplace daily occurrences in American schools. Effective education makes school-related violence less likely to occur, and that fact represents the real value of Dr. Brooks' *Violence*

Among Students and School Staff: Understanding and Preventing the Causes of School Violence. By presenting a comprehensive analysis of the causes of school-based violence, Dr. Brooks makes us better equipped to mitigate the effects of that violence.

The two students from Pinellas Park High School, Jason McCoy and Jason Harless, are now both out of prison. In 2012, the *Tampa Bay Times* contacted Harless and asked his thoughts regarding another high-profile school shooting: Sandy Hook Elementary School in Newtown, Connecticut. Harless, who served eight years in prison, expressed his repulsion over that incident, though he also said that "nothing" could prevent such horrors: "At the end of the day, there are no preventable measures. It's human nature" (Orlando, 2012).

It may be true that it is impossible to completely eliminate acts of violence in schools. But a more thorough understanding of the origins of such violence can equip teachers and the community at large to make schools safer for students. The work of Dr. Brooks is an important step toward that outcome.

Mark Pearcy, Ph.D.
Teacher Education Professor
Rider University

Preface

School violence is one subject that transcends time. While some may state that school violence is a timely subject and one worth investigating, it's evident that violence has been around since the birth of schooling. This is not a new phenomenon.

However, what is lacking is an education on the antecedents to school violence and an in-depth look at the factors and role players that contribute to this culture. With an emphasis in pre-service teacher training on lesson building, curriculum development, subject-knowledge acquisition, teacher leadership, and classroom management—violence prevention and conflict resolution strategies typically fall by the wayside. For example, Charmaraman, Jones, Stein, and Espelage (2012) report that roughly half of all current teachers report not receiving instruction on their district's policy for bullying and enforcement of such violent habits, while other teachers report not being able to distinguish between normal student behavior and bullying. Unfortunately, this lack of recognition and absence of education may begin within undergraduate pre-service teacher education programs.

Developmentally speaking, children and those within the adolescent stage of growth are at the highest risks of encountering different forms of violence. Serious health-related subjects are introduced to youth throughout these years and may become the precursors to violent behavior.

Figure 1: Different Forms of Violence (Center for Disease Control [CDC], 2013)

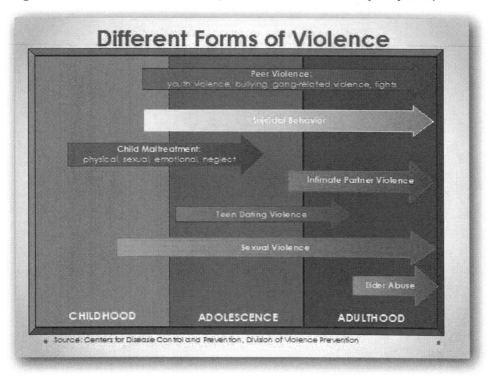

The CDC (2013) provides this figure to illustrate the factors that heavily contribute to a lack of student well-being. Late childhood shows a heightened exposure to forms of violent behavior, which progresses well through adolescence. These deeper-engrained behaviors can then easily travel well into adulthood. Again if these subjects are not taught formally within educational environments to both students and school staff, this absence of education may breed violent behavior. A school's staff that correctly and comprehensively addresses this fact may be more likely to prevent or reduce these associated behaviors.

It's specifically within the subject of K–12 health education where students can learn about conflict resolution, violent behaviors, and the accompanying factors that clearly impact childhood, adolescence, and adulthood. However, this education does not have to be singular to K–12 health education. College and university officials, educators, and students should also examine these factors (as school-related violence is not limited to K–12 schools). All school staff should address these subjects; particularly when they are suspected, witnessed, or directly reported within or around school environments. While this book primarily focuses on violence within K–12 environments, the similarities among all levels of education may be more evident than originally thought.

The North Carolina Department of Juvenile Justice and Delinquency Prevention's Center for the Prevention of School Violence (2002) defines school violence as "Any behavior that violates a school's educational mission or climate of respect or jeopardizes the intent of the school to be free of aggression against persons or property, drugs, weapons, disruptions, and disorder" (p. 1). Although this definition is older, it's within this very definition where the true problem of violence among school-aged children, adolescents, and those who work within such environments, are exposed.

So what happens when the schools themselves ignore such a definition, don't recognize it, or even worse, claim that students are the only ones to blame? What happens when a state of full denial and the "blame game" take over? For example, at the foundational level, many believe that when one enters the education profession, this alone becomes the universal qualifier to prevent and stop school-related violence. Teachers and school administrators may even comment on their status as parents and how this alone qualifies them to handle such violent situations among school-aged students. Or, how the number of years they have taught qualifies them to see violent behavior and prevent such actions from occurring. Such comments may carry little weight, as the simple act of reproducing does not qualify one to be a parent. Nor does the number of years one has taught qualify a person to prevent violence or properly recognize it. One act does not safeguard the other. Again, figure 1 above also illustrates how those within the stage of adulthood can be both the victims and perpetuators of diverse forms of violent behavior.

Students and school staff are exposed to many factors that are associated with violence, many of which have existed in the past and some of which are new in today's society. Espelage et al. (2013) state that intimidation, name-calling, and fighting are among the highest incidences of violent behavior in school, particularly among high-risk students (students who experience lower socioeconomic status, lower achievement levels). However, with the advancement of Internet communications and social media, no one is truly free from ridicule. Charmaraman et al. (2012) report in their study regarding school staff perceptions of violent behavior among students; that bullying can be remarkably high, as can workplace bullying among staff members, thereby giving students few role models to look up to with regard to preventing violent acts. Charmaraman et al. (2012) state that teachers also report not having enough resources to educate all students on a wide range of school violence prevention methods.

Socioeconomic factors, family responsibilities, developmental stages, divorce in the family, physical abilities, peer pressures, outdated school-sanctioned traditions, relationship pressures, drug and alcohol use, competition, and student-teacher connections can all contribute to violent behaviors that lead to unhealthy peer associations or unhealthy isolation. These dynamics can further compound a negative state of well-being that can lead to depression, self-harm, or the harm of other students and school staff. For example, Agnew (2001) states that anger and frustrating experiences can lead to crime and delinquency. Agnew (2005) also states that all humans are prone to frustrating and aggressive episodes or strain (general strain theory). This may lead to a dereliction of one's professional responsibilities or an increase in the likelihood of engaging in criminal activities (Agnew, 2005). When people remove themselves from their moral standards in order to justify an action, moral disengagement could become the norm, thereby leading to a perpetual downward slide of a moral conscience (Bandura, 2016). Moreover, some students and school staff may ultimately forget why they're really there.

Whether seen or unseen, the consequences of these behaviors can plague school environments, and an existing lack of qualifications among educators can compound present issues. Espelage, Low, and Jimerson (2014) describe the importance of education majors being professionally trained and training themselves, specifically in the social sciences, in order to address the needs of students and appropriately recognize and address the factors that contribute to bullying and harassment among students and school staff. Becoming consumers of relevant research can better prepare all educators for diverse classroom environments, while providing them the opportunity to examine their own beliefs regarding aggressive behavior (Espelage et al., 2014).

Professional educators, school administrators, and pre-service undergraduates are responsible for examining the true nature of school-related violence. Teachers must educate themselves regarding risk factors and prevention methods, and they should do so before they become classroom teachers. Waiting to learn about school violence until one becomes a classroom teacher may ultimately set oneself up for fail-ure. Waiting for a school district's professional-development session to handle such issues may be belated, impractical, and dangerous.

Experiences can be both educational and counterproductive depending on the quality of the experience (Dewey, 1938). Educators should drive the learning experi-ences of their learners; however, the quality of that education may be dependent on an educator's experiences (Dewey, 1938). This book aims to ignite the past education-al experiences of its readers and forge new paths of understating for increased states of awareness and preparedness.

The goals of this book are to examine the factors that contribute to school-relat-ed violence while making suggestions to prevent, reduce, and possibly eliminate the existing causes. I suggest having YouTube close by to access the embedded films that are included within this book. I also recommend reading this book more than twice. I hope you find it beneficial for your future success, and it's my hope that this informa-tion ultimately helps someone prevent violence among students and school staff.

1

The School Environment and School Climate

Two phrases are used in both research and school-evaluation methods regarding levels of safety and staff perceptions of their work environments. These phrases are *school environment* and *school climate*. The school environment refers to each and every component of a school's makeup that may contribute to a healthy or unhealthy learning environment and workplace. School environment is associated with the systems that exist inside of a school that may contribute to the buildings effectiveness or ineffectiveness, typically regarding policies and programs. Teachers, parents, students, and school staff are rarely asked about the quality of their school's environment. There may be good reasons why this is the case.

The school climate largely refers to how staff members feel about their working environment and whether they would consider it to be a healthy or happy place to work. School climate may rarely be surveyed, as this is sometimes only exclusive to scholarly research papers examining the perceptions of a school's staff. However, sometimes school staff members are asked to complete surveys regarding their own perceptions of their own school's environment or school's climate. Sometimes these surveys are shared with district officials. Sometimes they are ignored. The quality and obtainability of diverse perceptions of a school's environment and a school's climate may directly impact the levels of conflict and violence that exist within schools.

THE SCHOOL ENVIRONMENT

Evaluating a school's environment is essential for gaining knowledge that can help direct the behavior of students and school staff. For example, Johnson, Burke, and Gielen (2011) reported on student's perceptions of their school environment within a Baltimore City School district, among twenty-seven students. With regard to initial questioning, 50 percent of students reported being involved in a physical fight within the last twelve months (17 percent in group one; 33 percent in group two). Johnson et al. (2011) reported that bullying, relationship violence, and violence all over the building were concerns for students, and that these factors directly contributed to a poor school environment.

A frightening environment was also rated high among surveyed students. Students also reported that a poor school environment was related to their peers drawing attention to themselves, sexual behavior, drug use, sexual discrimination, and a lack of student maturity. These statements were all correlated to initiation, cessation, and severity of violent acts. Students also reported within this study that positive relationships with their teachers and the school staff would likely *not* improve the school's environment and an existing culture of violent behavior. Perhaps not surprisingly, this shows that once trust is broken, it's next to impossible to get back.

Johnson et al. (2011) stated that the primary role of the school environment is safety and the prevention of future violent acts. Students' overexposure to such factors could sap their will to succeed and negatively impact the human connections they make within a learning environment. Ultimately, such feelings could lead to a pessimistic cancer that impacts everyone within a school environment.

Richard, Schneider, and Mallet (2012) reported in their study regarding whole-school violence prevention, that the school environment is impacted by the relationships that students have with their teachers, along with the existence of shared feelings of safety and security. In France, where this study took place, students, teachers, and school principals participated in a survey across 478 schools predominantly made up of Caucasian students and teachers. Richard et al. (2012) stated that the higher-achieving schools with better student-teacher relationships were more likely to be safer and healthier learning environments.

However, students also largely reported that bullying and physical violence was likely to occur due to higher academic anxiety, impulsivity, and friendship conflicts. These very students reported being victims of bullying and physical intimidation more than other students. Peer acceptance was also associated with these types of violence within the school environment. Higher achieving students reported less physical abuse, but these higher achieving students also reported more verbal and relational abuse than their lower achieving classmates.

These results show that some students who are at the highest risks of violence within a school environment may be the higher achieving students within lower achieving schools. The same is true for lower achieving students in higher achieving schools (Richard et al., 2012). This study suggests that making approaches to educate the whole school, not just the victim or victimizer, may be a better approach than singling out students within a school environment as being solely responsible for the antecedents of violent behavior. Consistent evaluation of the whole school environment may ultimately expose these hidden causes of violence among both students and school staff.

THE SCHOOL CLIMATE

The school climate refers to the overall characteristics, quality, or feelings associated with a school's culture. Questions that address a school's climate may include the following: How well are the employees getting along? Would you recommend this working environment to someone else as a healthy place to educate students? In most situations, a school's environment is similar from building to building (class organization, activities, sports teams, clubs, staff positions, etc.). However, can this similar environmental makeup across many different landscapes be a contributing factor to aggression and violent behavior that negatively impacts a school's climate? Does a poor school environment ensure a poor school climate?

Espelage, Low, and Jimerson (2014) stated that when addressing a school's climate, one must unpack all dimensions of the existing environment and assess each through the eyes of the students, staff members, and the community—in order to reach the real reasons behind personal perceptions. Depending on a school's administration, a school's climate may never be evaluated. However, if administered, these surveys might not ask the appropriate questions that lead to a direct link to violent behavior among students and school staff. Such surveys might only address one's willingness to work in, or recommend the school to outsiders. These surveys are typically formatted with a rating of the school's climate on a scale of one to ten.

Espelage et al. (2014) stated that violent behavior and positive prevention methods can also be addressed within climate surveys, but only if the school's climate is evaluated in a formal and thorough way. Only then can perceptions, knowledge, and beliefs about violent behavior be examined. Such thorough examinations can meet the needs of students' mental, emotional, social and physical health, motivational levels, and academic achievement.

Student perceptions of their school's climate have been shown to both predict and prevent aggressive behavior (White, La Salle, Ashby, & Meyers, 2014). Such results have also been shown to predict and positively adjust academic achievement. When students and community members are directly involved in a school's climate survey, school districts and their communities may better address the needs of their youth. Not including student and community feedback on the surrounding learning environments or school's climate might simply equate to not asking a typical customer about his or her experience. In the interest of continuous improvement, schools exist to serve the students and the community. Ultimately students, their families, and the surrounding communities are the intended customers.

STUDENT PERCEPTIONS OF THEIR LEARNING ENVIRONMENTS

As described earlier, students in different learning environments differ in their perceptions of school-related violence. Sometimes this depends on the geographic location of a classroom within a school, the student's relationships to peers, or the student's previous education or personal experiences with school staff members. For example, Alvarez, Farmer, Bessette, Shaunessy-Dedrick, and Ray (2014) explored middle school students' perceptions of their learning environments based on drawings. The school environments include gifted classrooms, special education classrooms, and general education classrooms. Students were then prompted to draw the classroom environment, their teacher's characteristics, and the characteristics of their fellow peers. In almost every student-drawn depiction of their learning environment, students characterized their peers agreeing with them regarding a perceived negative tone among their teachers. Throughout the majority of the drawings, students illustrated words coming from teachers, such as *shut up, work harder, finish the work I gave you*, and, yelling the word, *quiet!* Perhaps the most telling comment is in figure 5, where the student states that the teacher makes school "like a slow and painful death." Below are illustrated examples from that very study.

4

Figure 2: Investigating Middle-School Students' Perceptions of Their Learning Environments Through Drawings (Alvarez, Farmer, Bessette, Shaunessy-Dedrick, & Ray, 2014)

Figure 3:

Figure 4:

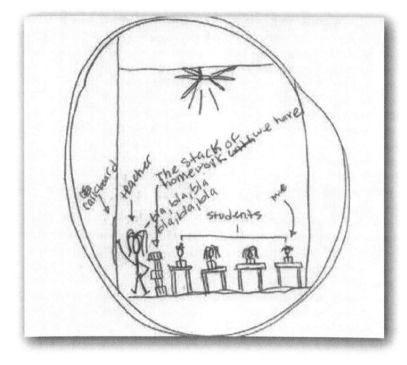

Figure 5:

In each depiction drawn by middle school students, the teacher comes across as overbearing and dominant. However, there are some drawings that occurred in the study that showed the teacher positively engaging the students, and the students enjoying the teacher's positive levels of enthusiasm. Students also verbally reported specific positive behaviors to the researchers. Students claimed that enthusiasm; positive energy, charisma, and knowledge of the subject matter were all traits that made up a positive student experience (Alvarez et al., 2014).

What continues to be fascinating about allowing students to draw their perceptions of their learning environments is the insight it can provide about how students may feel about classroom-related emotions. Such drawings are rarely conducted. Examining this approach further may provide insight into how emotions generated from the teachers toward their students, and vice versa, can be a major factor in students' perception of their teachers and their personal learning environment. This practice could even be adopted within school environment or school climate evaluations. However, such a practice would most likely not exist, due to fearing the truth. As an education specialist at a professional conference once told me "Youth-truth is the most telling, and many don't want to hear it."

The school environment can have a dramatic impact on a student's well-being and overall health. The routines, traditions, and structures that are widely adopted in schools can create an environment of student dissatisfaction. Jamal, Fletcher, Harden, Wells, Thomas, and Bonell (2013) concluded that these very structures in place may lead to higher student aggression, thereby giving way to more permissive behaviors such as negative peer associations, drug use, and an overall lack of focus on academics.

What school officials believe to be healthy contributors to a school's learning environment, may actually be the cause of negative health among the student population. Jamal et al., (2013) suggests giving students choices to increase their overall health while at school, while avoiding forced student participation. For example, school cafeterias are notorious for gossip and other student-driven negative behaviors. Ironically, this takes place in the very environment where an attempt to promote positive well-being through healthy food and healthy socialization is widely adopted. Jamal et al. (2013) state that giving students the freedom to eat with teachers, with plenty of space, or in a healthier location (i.e., classrooms) might decrease peer aggression. In the end, giving students more of a decision-making voice may benefit the whole school environment and the school's climate.

SUMMARY POINTS FOR CHAPTER 1

- School environments and the way they are structured are key contributors to a negative and potentially violent learning environment.
- Student perceptions of their schools, their classrooms, and their teachers may play a role in lower academic success and create unnecessary division.
- The very school structures and routines that are in place may lead to higher student aggression, thereby giving way to more permissive behaviors, such as negative peer associations, drug use, and an overall lack of focus on academics.
- When addressing a school's climate, one must unpack all the dimensions of the existing environment and assess each through the eyes of the students, staff members, and the community in order to reach the real reasons behind current perceptions.
- Students' perceptions of their school's climate have been shown to both predict and prevent aggressive behavior. Such results have also been shown to predict academic achievement.
- Asking students what they think about their school's environment, their teachers, and their administrators can shed a light on the quality of communication among all parties.

2

The Mental and Emotional Health
of Students and School Staff

The World Health Organization (WHO, 2001) describes mental and emotional health as a state of well-being in which the individual realizes his or her own abilities, can cope with the normal stresses of life, can work productively and fruitfully, and is able to make a contribution to his or her own community. More specifically, the CDC (2013) describes depression as the biggest mental and emotional health problem impacting our society. It should be noted that with each professional diagnosis of a condition, many more cases go undiagnosed. Among those professionally diagnosed, many of them are over-diagnosed and misdiagnosed as well. This misinformation can be remarkably common among those working within school environments.

With so many life changes during these developmental years, a child may be more likely to suffer from depressive thoughts, aggression, and anger than anything else. The shifting school environment, family life, pressures at school, and social influences are all likely to contribute to a decline in a student's frame of mind. The adults within school environments must play the role of a preventive mentor rather than instigator.

However, teachers and school officials are also not free from the factors that lead to a decline in mental health. Shifting roles, increased responsibilities, disillusionment, job stress, poor school leadership, political influence, shifting evaluation methods, and negative feelings regarding a lack of acceptance; can all lead school staff members to decline mentally and emotionally. Such factors can cause school employees to leave the education profession altogether, or to remain in their position with a potentially undiagnosed illness. Drug addiction, binge drinking, overeating, a lack of exercise, and poor sleep habits can all be side effects of an educator suffering from a poor work environment. Any failure to prevent these symptoms can have a negative impact on teachers, their students, school administrators, the classroom environment, and a school's overall culture of learning.

With depression and the associated conditions a real issue for school-aged students and school staff, what are the short-term and long-term impacts of such illnesses? I want to examine the impact that schools can have on the conditions associated with mental and emotional health, and the methods through which everyone can remedy these conditions.

DEPRESSION AMONG SCHOOL-AGED STUDENTS

Perhaps the most hidden issue among school-aged students involves the impact that school officials, families, and peers can have on the occurrences of childhood depression. The National Institute of Mental Health (NIMH, 2015) reports that depression among children, like many other individuals, could come as a singular event or a combination of genetic and environmental factors that cause moods to swing. These chemical imbalances that lead to depressive episodes can begin in early childhood and can carry well into adulthood if not recognized or left untreated. Females in particular are twice as likely, after roughly age fifteen, to suffer from depression than males (NIMH, 2015).

Pratt and Brody (2008) reported in their brief, that more than one out of every twenty Americans, twelve years of age and older, reported current depression in 2005–2006. It could be that environmental factors play the biggest role in student-aged depression, given the number of students in school, the changing classroom environments, expectations, academic pressures, and changing relationships that characterize the lives of children and adolescents within school.

McDougall (2011) addressed how nurses can better attend to children with mental and emotional disorders, and how professional help can give children relief regarding such serious conditions. Upon further examination in table 1 below, McDougall's (2011) list is one that anyone can discuss with school-aged students.

Table 1: Ways to Promote Resilience in Children and Adolescents (McDougall, 2010)

1. Think positively and be optimistic: people have little or no control over negative events, but they can influence how they feel about them.
2. Take a different perspective: there are many different ways to consider things.
3. Embrace challenges: things that at first may seem difficult may be easy to overcome.
4. Do something to help someone else: pro-social behavior such as community involvement helps build resilience.
5. Encourage play and creativity: this enables children and young people to learn about themselves, their relationships with others, and the world around them.
6. Identify and nurture strengths: by recognizing positive qualities and reinforcing them, children will grow in self-esteem, pride, and confidence.
7. Promote self-esteem and self-efficacy: these are the fundamental building blocks of resilience and can be enhanced by participating in valued activities.
8. Make connections: good relationships create a climate of support.
9. Explore opportunities for self-discovery: children who have expressed trauma or loss often grow and develop as a result of their experiences. This can stand them in good stead for dealing with future stress.
10. Look after yourself: eat healthily, sleep properly, and exercise regularly. Looking after themselves helps people to keep their mind and body resilient.

If teachers, parents, and school administrators took the time to address these strategies and find ways of implementing them within the home and within classroom instruction, students may feel less controlled by the school environment. Perhaps it's the absence of this education that may be a leading cause of student-related depression. With the combination of a negative social stigma regarding mental health, and a school's need to succeed academically and be free of violence, school administrators and teachers should recognize the true causes of depression among school-aged students. Any denial regarding the presence of depression among school-aged students and school staff members may create the very characteristics that lead to destructive mental and emotional disorders.

Drug use, sexual promiscuity, failed relationships, thoughts of suicide, lowered academic involvement, lowered academic success, self-harming, and social withdrawal; are all byproducts of mental disorders like depression. If students know someone who is depressed in their school, they may attach to that person and their habits to feel a sense of belonging. This may occur even if those habits are harmful, thereby potentially propagating mental illness between both parties. The National Institute of Mental Health (1985) specifically states that depression affects one out of five teenage students at some point in their lives. I would argue that this number is now drastically higher.

The CDC (2015) reports that those who have a depressive episode early in life are at a higher risk of encountering multiple depressive episodes, roughly 50 percent more likely. The CDC (2015) also suggests that depression could be easily linked to other adverse health effects that may prolong depression in an individual, such as drug use, smoking, alcohol consumption, physical inactivity, poor eating habits, and sleep disturbances. All of these factors are likely to be introduced within the adolescent years of a student's life. These factors are also easily observable among students within a school environment.

The role of the teacher in appropriately addressing these matters is of the upmost importance. Sadly most teachers never receive education or training on mental disorders, or the recognition that's necessary for spotting the warning signs among school-aged students. Therefore, the chances of teachers actually teaching prevention methods to their students are unlikely. This is a major contributor as to why so many mental and emotional illnesses go largely unreported among school-aged students. The lack of awareness among teachers and school administrators may force the student's hand in dealing with his or her problems alone. This may drive the student deeper into the unhealthy habits that exacerbate a disorder.

King and Vidourek (2012) describe warning signs of teen depression and suggest that the key components to preventing such disorders should come from an awareness of those around the individual in recognizing the signs and symptoms. Table 2 highlights examples of warning signs associated with the possible onset, or current existence of teenage depression.

Table 2: Teen Depression Warning Signs (King & Vidourek, 2012)

1. Experiencing sadness, unhappiness, and crying spells
2. Feeling restless and agitated
3. Having difficulty sleeping or sleeping successfully
4. Feeling fatigued
5. Showing irritability
6. Possessing feelings of shame, guilt or worthlessness
7. Feeling bored most or all of the time
8. Having a loss of interest in once pleasurable activities
9. Having problems with concentration, memory, and decision-making
10. Moving and talking slowly
11. Experiencing sudden weight loss or weight gain
12. Having thoughts of death or suicide (morbid ideation)

I would add to the list above by having school staff be aware of the physical signs that are potentially driven by the existence of a mental illness such as:

- Change in skin tone (possible drug use)
- Bruising on the face, legs, and backs of the arms
- Visible hickies (signs of sexual promiscuity)
- Track marks (signs of drug use)
- Cut marks or scaring on thighs, arms, lower legs or hands
- Poor hygiene or unkempt appearance
- Isolation
- Lack of eye contact
- Disinterested facial expressions
- Sharp tone of voice, yelling or irrational responses to simple questions
- Eczema, bleeding or tearing of the flesh
- Nervous or fidgety habits (eating pencils, eating paper)
- Pulling hair from the body; having missing hair or bald spots (trichotillomania)

Untreated depression and anxiety are the leading causes of suicide among teen-agers (King & Vidourek, 2012). School staff should be educated on such serious and common mental and emotional health conditions, particularly teenage depression and anxiety. Students themselves should also be taught these related subjects, so that they too can identify the common risk factors within themselves or their fellow peers.

THE MENTAL AND EMOTIONAL HEALTH OF TEACHERS AND SCHOOL STAFF

As stated before, teachers and other school staff are not free from mental and emo-tional fatigue or associated illnesses. This is not just an issue for students. Stress among educators is a major contributor to a variety of unhealthy associated habits. Overeating, a lack of exercise, alcohol consumption, stressful home life, heightened aggression, prescription drug abuse, poor sleep habits, and increased social confron-tations; are just some of the factors stemming from increased stress levels among educators.

Amelia Hill of the *Guardian* (2008) wrote an article describing many contributing factors to higher stress levels among educators. She stated that based on a YouGov survey in 2007, roughly half of all teachers have considered quitting because of stress. A lack of respect from pupils and coworkers, heavy workload, and abrasive parents—are all reasons for quitting. It is also referenced in the *Guardian* article that one in three teachers relied on alcohol, drugs, and binge eating to cope with stress, while some had suicidal thoughts as a result of school-related demands.

Even though this information was gathered in England, the same can be said here in America. Adding to the above examples, the politicization of education has taken away the philosophy of teaching and made it a political topic far from a teacher's con-trol. It's possible that fewer and fewer teachers are considering becoming schoolteach-ers or administrators due to the added stress associated with such positions.

These added pressures within an educational position can take a toll on the economy as well. Teachers and administrators take off hundreds of thousands of days from working throughout a school year due to anxiety, depression, and stress. This can cost countries hundreds of millions of dollars in lost productivity while substi-tutes and unqualified adults are hired to temporarily or permanently fill in. Within the *Guardian* article, Stan Gilmore of the Institute of Counseling is quoted as saying, "Most teachers, if they are honest, will testify that at some point in their teaching career they have encountered difficulties in coping with the relentless pressure to maintain order, leading to the kind of emotional exhaustion colloquially known as a mental break-down." The *Guardian* article stated that 40 percent of teachers would be leaving their teaching jobs within the first five years due to added stress and mental and emotional breakdowns.

Students in teacher education undergraduate programs should be educated on how to manage such situations, recognize them, and work to avoid such unpleasant workplace elements. They should understand of course, that control over their work environment might be hard at times, as more and more pressures are put on teachers to force positive achievement and positive behavior out of their students. However, compassionate and healthy learning environments are what allow for high levels of achievement from all, including school staff. Teaching pre-service teachers to take care of themselves physically, mentally, emotionally, and socially—and to recognize any onset of these health problems, may be a logical first step.

TEACHER BURNOUT

Teacher burnout is defined as disengagement, fatigue, and stress-related factors associated with teaching (Pas, Bradshaw, Hershfeldt, & Leaf, 2010). Teacher burnout can have major implications regarding the levels of both personal and school related violence. For example, Pas et al. (2010) reported that higher rates of teacher burnout might also contribute to a less-enforced discipline policy for students. Pas et al. (2010) stated that this gives way to a higher probability of problematic student behaviors, with lower levels of teacher intervention and student accountability. With time, increased fatigue, and increased school or student disorder, teachers may rely more heavily on discipline policies for managing student infractions or they may ignore discipline altogether (Pas et al., 2010). Underlying personal-health problems may lead to a reluctance or unwillingness to engage in student situations that immediately require a teacher's attention. Any lack of involvement with preventing school-related violence would most certainly lead to more violence.

The healthy mindedness of teachers can decrease the amount of violence within classrooms and within school environments. If teachers are aware of their own negative frames of mind, avoiding irrational confrontations will decrease school-related conflicts and foster a more positive learning environment. There is no doubt that teacher dissatisfaction and disillusionment can lead to negative confrontations with students and decrease healthy teaching. Therefore, addressing these stressors with licensed professionals can provide relief so that students don't suffer from the effects of an unhealthy educator.

SUMMARY POINTS FOR CHAPTER 2

- Mental illness, particularly depression, impacts students in school, teachers, and school staff alike.
- Depression among children, like individuals of other ages, can come as a singular event or a combination of genetic and environmental factors that cause moods to swing.
- Depression can be easily linked to other adverse health effects that may create and prolong depression in an individual, such as drug use, smoking, alcohol consumption, physical inactivity, poor eating habits, and sleep disturbances.
- Compassionate learning environments will allow for high levels of achievement from all, including the school staff.
- Higher rates of teacher burnout (defined as disengagement, fatigue, and stress-related factors associated with teaching) may contribute to a less enforced discipline policy, therefore giving way for a higher probability of problematic student behaviors with lower levels of teacher intervention and student accountability.
- The healthy mindedness of a teacher will decrease the amount of violence within a classroom and a school environment.
- Removing oneself from an unhealthy work environment and finding a new location to work may also increase the healthy mindfulness of a school staff member. If a poor work environment is a major contributor to the decline of one's own mental and emotional health, changing environments may be the best option.

3

Frustration, Aggression, and Bullying

In his book of compiled essays and experiments, *The Individual in a Social World*, Stanley Milgram (1992) states that when we as humans submit to authority we tend to remove ourselves from the thought of personal responsibility. This tends to occur even when we hold positions where we are sworn to defend the well-being of individuals. For example, if school-level administrators and teachers fail to recognize or enforce the antecedents to frustration, aggression, and bullying among students or staff members, the realistic expectations of a safe environment can become absent. As Agnew (2011) states, it's within these many forms of communication between youth and adults where frustration and aggression can arise from the feelings associated with unjust behavior.

As bullying is commonly discussed in twenty-four hour news cycles, the causes of bullying are rarely examined publically. Professionals in the media rarely interview educators themselves about these topics. Instead, a therapist may be called upon to discuss an issue, or a lawyer is invited to provide his or her opinion. With regard to bullying and its predecessors frustration and aggression, we as a society may heavily rely on the unqualified opinions of others to shape our beliefs. When looking for the correct causes and solutions to frustration, aggression, and bullying in school—I recommend starting with K–12 educators who have taught conflict resolution or violence prevention. It's with these individuals that education, combined with experience, may lead to the most realistic school-based solutions.

STUDENT FRUSTRATION AND AGGRESSION

When we examine aggressive behavior, there are many factors that contribute to such an emotional stimulation. Home life, parental behavior, poverty, environmental or locational quality, money, intellect, peer pressure, family history of aggression, learned behaviors, abuse, and legal trouble; are all contributing factors—most of which can't be controlled by school-aged students. This is why the practices implemented by teachers and administrators need to remove any threatening behavior, so one doesn't contribute to its growth. Failure to do so may only create more frustrated students, thereby increasing their levels of personal, social, mental, emotional, and physical aggression.

Blair (2010) examined the definitions of frustration and aggression, and their links to one another. This research goes back decades, as many psychologists have looked at the antecedents to frustration and aggression. Specifically, Blair (2010) summarized that frustration leads to aggression, and the more aggressive one becomes overtime due to increased frustration stimuli, the more an individual's brain can lead to what's referred to as *reversal learning* or *behavioral extinction*. For example, positive behaviors may be replaced by negative aggressive behaviors over time, as the frustration levels of humans are increased or stimulated with regularity. The same is true regarding academic achievement and a student's willingness to succeed. This motivation or desire to achieve can be wiped clean from a student's mind when they are subjected to repetitious frustration.

In an innovative study, Gome-Garibello, Sayka, Moore, and Talwar (2013) examined the abilities of teachers to recognize lying among children who were describing situations of bullying they had experienced. The adult observers were shown video footage of school children, aged from infancy to twelve years old, describing experiences with bullying. Some children were coached beforehand to lie, while others were told to tell the truth. The participating adult observers included pre-service teachers, daycare workers, and elementary school teachers, aged nineteen to sixty-five, 90 percent of whom were female. The results showed that pre-service teachers were more likely than daycare workers to hold a truth bias, as they believed students more readily when describing episodes of bullying.

The authors concluded that an adult's age was not a determining factor in an educator's ability to accurately or confidently assess a student's truthfulness. Teachers at each level both accurately and inaccurately assessed eight videotaped children, and the results showed that their surveyed determinations were not above the level of chance. Beforehand, each group (pre-service teachers, daycare workers, and elementary school teachers) firmly believed that they would be able to accurately detect those students who were lying, from those students who were telling the truth about being bullied. This clearly shows that experience and age are not determining factors in assessing honesty among students, in particular when it comes to violent behavior. This may directly contribute to strain between students and teachers regarding the fair and accurate handling of bullying and discipline in or around school environments, as both victims and victimizers can be falsely accused and punished unfairly while the entire school population watches.

Fives, Kong, Fuller, and DiGiuseppe (2011) conducted a study among 135 high-school students to measure their perceptions of aggression. According to the study, when it came to the interpretation of school rules, frustration and aggression increased among students. The students also reported that physical aggression was more likely to occur among males than females. Both sexes shared the perception that frustration related to rules within school, directly increased their levels of physical aggression and advanced their frustration. Fives et al. (2011) stated that any attempt to reduce irrational beliefs and increase rational beliefs among students might positively influence the prevention of childhood and adolescent anger and aggression.

While Fives et al. (2011) suggest that clinical professionals should examine these results and work to figure out treatment approaches, I would state that the responsibility lies with teachers and administrators within schools to clarify all information, and consistently address the school-related factors that may increase such frustration and aggression levels, before they start. This leads me to a classroom related destructive practice I refer to as *classroom instructional aggression*.

CLASSROOM INSTRUCTIONAL AGGRESSION

While this practice has not been scientifically proven in scholarly research, I would presume that any student within a school environment could be directly or indirectly lead by his or her teacher to become frustrated, thereby leading to student aggression. Specifically, *classroom instructional aggression* refers to any classroom or school practice, lead by teachers or administrators, that may seek to trick, divide, punish, create hostility and anxiety, and manipulate or deceive a student or group of students, intentionally or unintentionally, under the guise of instruction. For example, within a classroom environment, homework or schoolwork administered by teachers to their students may be used as a punishment or as a weapon to encourage compliance (i.e., "Because you're not being quiet, instead of ten math problems due tomorrow, you now have thirty!"). Not only does this fail to motivate the student to comply or academically achieve, but this practice also tends to frustrate the entire group of students within the classroom, thereby leading to the likelihood of aggressive thoughts toward the class subject, teacher, or the school as a whole.

Other examples include, but are not limited to the following:

- Pop quizzes (quizzes given by a teacher to students at a moments notice without prior warning)
- Student-versus-student academic competition designed by the school or teacher
- Classroom-versus-classroom academic competition designed by the school or teacher
- Competition between grade levels
- Removal from a learning environment to attend a non-learning environment where some student successes are highlighted while others may be diminished (pep rallies, sporting events, dances, student-council voting/activities)
- Displaying of students' individual or group grades in front of the whole class (not privately sharing grades between the teacher and the student; asking a students to say out loud how many answers they have right or wrong for the teacher's ease of recording grades)
- Completion of schoolwork in front of the whole class by one student, particularly when knowledge is not known about the subject or a lesson has just begun (forcing students to solve math problems publically, in front of the whole class)
- Unfair distribution of rewards (some students receive recognition while other deserve it as well)

- Favoritism by educators before, during or after class (among those who academically succeed, student athletes, students associated with school cliques)
- The teacher singling out students who have nothing to contribute or choose to not participate
- Counting participation as a grade
- Making students dress out (take their cloths off) in physical-education class in front of their peers and giving them a lower grade due to noncompliance
- Foreign-language instructors speaking in the foreign language they are teaching when the students do not know the language (specifically when assignments are described or directions are given)
- Forcing students to read out loud, in large sections at a time, regardless of their disabilities, speech impediments, and so on
- Forcing students to read outdated fiction books or specific genres of literature when non-fiction may be preferred
- Holding debates in classrooms on critical social or political issues where student or teacher opinions can become hostile
- Forcing student participation during science dissections when students feel uncomfortable (dissecting animals: cats, rabbits, fetal pigs, etc.)
- Unfair or bigoted distribution of punishments (one race or gender receives a punishment, while another gets away with the same behavior or action)
- Icebreaker games that force students to ask probing or personal questions to their peers
- Scavenger hunts, where direct instruction is absent and time is wasted
- Playing name-recognition games where students learn everyone's names in class (students sit in rows and are forced to recall past students' names before publically introducing themselves)
- Allowing students to pick groups or teams (someone being left out because of physical appearance, intellect or disability)
- Having poor feedback timing with the returning of assignments (poor timing or returning work late; poor rubrics that fail to define why a student received a particular grade)

- Giving assignments to students to be completed over the weekends, holidays, snow days or spring and summer vacations
- Unfair lengths of assignments or tests (providing assignments or tests that are too long to complete in the allotted time or too time-consuming that a subsequent activity can never be accomplished)
- Teachers failing to take time and define the grading system (not teaching students about grade percentages, assignment point distribution, etc.)
- Using nicknames with students instead of their birth names or appropriate names they wish to be called
- School popularity contests (prom king/queen, homecoming king/queen, student-council positions, superlative contests). These also set the table for a student with a disability to be taken advantage of publically and voted for when perhaps that student did not want to participate.
- Classroom or school-based segregation based on disability or academic achievement level

While small doses of anxiety may help engage some students in some learning situations, most people reading this list would agree that they have been victims of such practices and behaviors within classrooms and schools. Some habits mentioned above are also more likely to exist in some classes more than others, due to their subject matter (i.e., debating about political issues in social studies class). Therefore, specific classroom subjects can illicit specific aggressive instructional methods and aggressive student responses that may be particular to that subject or learning environment.

School staff members can also administer these aggressive practices, or ones like them, upon their fellow coworkers. For example, in an effort to obtain compliance or control a situation, administrators or teachers may use similar aggressive tactics within faculty meetings or other moments of group assembly. The above practices also commonly demean the intellect of participants. It is within these very practices that students and school staff are likely to feel frustrations that lead to aggression, thereby increasing the potential for a hostile act. We also know that people are likely to act out in two different ways when frustrations or aggressions show themselves. First, individuals can act out through self-directed violent behavior (cutting, self-harm, drug use, alcohol abuse, and sexual promiscuity) or second, individuals can act out

22

toward those outside of themselves (physical aggression, threats, fighting, name-calling, harassment, sexual aggression). One directed form of abuse could also easily lead to another. A complete removal of these methods mentioned as components of classroom instructional aggression, would certainly create a safer and more objective learning environment.

DEFINING BULLYING

The birth of the modern use of the word *bullying* is thought to have originated in the mid-to-late 1700s. The word and the definition have not gone away with time. As it turns out, the name has taken on new and serious meanings, and laws have been created around the very definition of this word. The CDC (2013) defines bullying as "A form of youth violence that can be inflicted physically, verbally, socially (i.e., spreading rumors), or by damaging a young person's property. It can harm a young person physically, emotionally, and academically. Beyond the individual, bullying can hurt peers, families, schools, and neighborhoods." This very definition is missing one major point of fact. Bullying is not limited to *youth*. All people regardless of age can perpetuate this hate-filled act.

The CDC's (2013) Youth Risk Behavior Survey (YRBS) reports that roughly 20 percent of high school students reported being bullied on school property in a year's time, while roughly 25 percent of middle school students (grades six through eight) reported being bullied at school in 2013. Given what we know about bullying thus far, and about how teachers and administrators can perpetuate such acts, I would argue that bullying occurs every day in the lives of every student, directly or indirectly, publically or privately. Rates of bullying are commonly reported at a rate of 25 percent. This percentage is far too low. The real prevalence of bullying is closer to 100 percent. No one is free from ridicule or torment, publically or privately, directly or indirectly.

With many forms of bullying existing, the types of bullying and the locations where these acts occur in school, also require a firm examination. Perkins, Perkins, and Craig (2014) surveyed twenty middle schools inside New York and New Jersey. Students participated in an online survey where they answered questions related to bullying and victimization, and the locations where such episodes occurred. Figure 6 below shows the results of the types of bullying and victimization that students reported.

Figure 6: Victimization Types (Ways Harassed/Bullied) in Last Thirty Days: (a) Prevalence of Type by Sex, (b) Frequency of Type (Perkins, Perkins, & Craig, 2014)

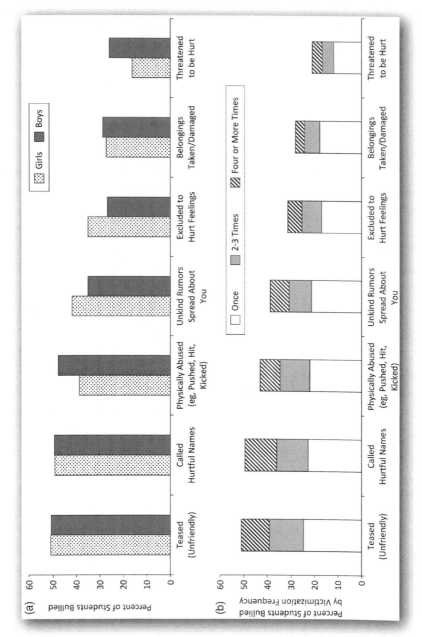

It's clear that teasing, name-calling, and physical abuse continue to be the top three most common forms of bullying. What is also not surprising is what was discovered about specific locations within schools and their connections to bullying and victimization. The students reported that the top seven locations where bullying and victimization are likely to occur are hallways, classrooms, lunchrooms, gymnasiums, buses, playgrounds, and bathrooms. While school personnel can monitor these locations within a school setting, most go unsupervised and unmonitored, thereby leading to an increase in student victimization. Perkins et al. (2014) reported that teasing and name-calling top the list of the most common forms of bullying within these locations. They state that physical violence is the number-one reported type of bullying within hallways, gymnasiums, and the playground. Turning a blind eye to such behavior or locations only sets the table for further bullying to exist, thereby making victimization worse.

Given that bullying takes many forms and exists within every school, stating otherwise may be an absence of acknowledging the truth while perpetuating a state of denial that ultimately hurts those who inhabit a school environment. Situational intervention is a necessity when frustration, aggression, or bullying is seen or heard. While not every incident of bullying can be caught or dealt with appropriately or in a timely fashion, they all should be. Perhaps even more revealing is how schoolteachers and administrators largely supervise these very hostile areas. If the environments themselves cannot be properly supervised, perhaps a removal of such environments, activities, or personnel—can decrease the likelihood of such violent acts.

The below web address is a video compilation of school-related fights, bullying, and student deaths attributed to violence in and around school. I suggest familiarizing yourself with these situations and imagining how you would respond in a preventive and reactionary manner.

- https://www.youtube.com/watch?v=SuowQ4UXVx8
- YouTube Search Title: *Fatal high school fight: teen cleared in single punch death, school bully killed - compilation*

BULLYING OF LGBTQ STUDENTS

Not a single student attends school to be hurt. Every student wants to learn in a safe environment free of prejudice beliefs and discrimination. Students who are lesbian, gay, bisexual, transgender, or questioning can be ridiculed in school if they are assumed to be, associated with, or are identified as such. Sometimes violence associated with these students can find their way to local newspapers and nationally televised news channels. Sadly, many more bullying cases go unreported and uninvestigated among all students regardless of any categorization.

Mueller, James, Abrutyn, and Levin (2015) reported that those students who identify as LGBTQ are just as likely to be victimized as their fellow peers, regardless of race, sexual orientation, or age. The same is true with suicidal ideation. So, it could be stated that bullying does not single out one group or another.

The frequency of deaths attributed to suicide by LGBTQ students, because of bullying, is also rarely recorded; as such identifying and specific factors may not be present on death certificates (i.e., bullied to death). We know that this mistreatment may lead to suicidal ideation as well as the mental and emotional trauma that comes with added ridicule in a school, or within online environments. Addressing media literacy and professionalism with all students and school staff members may give LGBTQ students, and frankly all students, the best shot at navigating what can be a notoriously unhealthy school behavior.

In a study conducted by Kolbert, Crothers, Bundick, Wells, Buzgon, Berbary, and Senko (2015), the authors distributed a survey across a Southwestern section of a Midwestern state, across forty-two school districts. Two hundred and seventeen different educators completed at least a portion of the survey. The study examined the perceptions of teachers with regard to LGBTQ student experiences and teachers' experiences with regard to violence directed toward these students. As with other forms of violence, the more these teachers identified with LGBTQ students, the more teachers recognized bullying. The less teachers recognized LGBTQ students and their potential struggles, the less these teachers recognized bullying within their classrooms and schools.

Similar perceptions were made with regard to how teachers identified themselves. Kolbert et al. (2015) discovered that among teachers who were considered heterosexual, their LGBTQ coworkers viewed them as being less observant of bullying among LGBTQ students. When asked about the schools environment and protection of all students including LGBTQ students, heterosexual teachers were more likely to state that the school environment supported all students equally. Clearly, a school employee's perception is everything, and differing perceptions of hostility can create division between students and school staff.

The polarizing nature of some school communities can also contribute to a lack of awareness with regard to victimization of some groups of students over others.

While heterosexual students are less likely to be tormented for being heterosexual, LGBTQ students are likely to be bullied, harassed, called names, and physically assaulted due to their sexual or gender identification in K–12 schools. Clearly, teacher and administrative perceptions vary regarding the issues of bullying across all students and especially those who identify as LGBTQ students.

Kitchen and Bellini (2012) stated that teacher perceptions in appropriately handling LGBTQ issues in school is directly associated with a lack of education that occurs within teacher education programs for pre-service candidates. Kitchen and Bellini (2012) reported that after a two-hour workshop within a teacher education program, teacher candidates reported a higher ability to appropriately handle issues of bullying and harassment among LGBTQ students within school environments. Even with this example being considered an ineffective dose-effect approach (small amounts of information shared in a one-time meeting), it's clear that more education needs to exist within teacher education programs and K–12 schools regarding any topic that addresses student violence. As teacher candidates enter diverse school populations, their future students are relying on their teachers to be vigilant in preventing and addressing violence among all students.

In an editorial written by Wiederhold (2014), they reported that students who identify as LGBTQ are more likely to be bullied and harassed in online environments than their heterosexual peers. Wiederhold (2014) also reported that a study by the Gay, Lesbian, and Straight Education Network (GLSEN) stated that LGBTQ students were more likely to use the Internet on a daily basis (forty-five minutes longer) than their heterosexual peers. As it turns out, the method of escaping to an online environment to find *peace* may ultimately be counterproductive. Removing oneself from social-media outlets may be a quick answer to reducing and ending victimization among all students, including LGBTQ students. Such communication methods and a simple curiosity about how our peers are socializing about us can lead to victimization, bullying, depression, anxiety, and thoughts of suicide.

Schoolteachers and their administrators often use poor programs and intellectually insulting assemblies to focus on students accepting the differences they have with one another. Perhaps schools should focus on the similarities among humans, as these are always more interesting and abundant. It's the categorizing of violence and hate into differing groups or arbitrary titles that can reproduce and perpetuate more violence and hate.

SUMMARY POINTS FOR CHAPTER 3

- Frustration leads to aggression, and the more aggressive one becomes over time due to increased frustration stimuli, the more an individual's brain can lead to what's referred to as *reversal learning* or *behavioral extinction*.

- Any attempt to reduce irrational beliefs and increase rational beliefs among students may positively influence the prevention of childhood and adolescent frustration and aggression.

- *Classroom instructional aggression* and the associated factors may contribute to an increase in student frustration, aggression, and bullying behavior among all parties within school environments. Removal of these poor practices is essential.

- Teasing and name-calling top the list as the most common forms of bullying, while physical violence is the number-one reported type of victimization within hallways, gymnasiums, and the playground.

- Educated teachers, administrators or national researchers who have a specific background in violence prevention in school should handle training and professional development within school districts. Proven facts should be presented.

- Teachers should remain in contact through parent-teacher meetings with pupils' parents or guardians. Teachers should monitor students' friendship patterns as well.

- All schools should be encouraged to establish some kind of peer-support systems with the help of educators, parents or school psychologists and other professionals.

- Teachers, professionals, and relevant authorities should develop a system of monitoring the causes of frequent student absences from school.

- All students can be the victims of bullying in school and over the Internet regardless of their categorization.

- Teacher perceptions must evolve regarding the harassment and bullying of all students. Teachers and administrators must be observant of these occurrences. Education about preventing and dealing with bullying must start at the undergraduate level of teacher education and continue throughout the whole teaching career.

Social-Media Use and Cyberbullying

With the advent of social media in American culture and its presence within other media formats, students are pressured to participate. Either directly or indirectly, school-aged students are no matches for the pseudo-importance that can be placed on the use of social media. Students in kindergarten can have Facebook and Twitter accounts, as they are quickly branded with a societal pressure to use social media at an early and influential age. While YouTube, Skype, BrainPop. com, Google Classroom, and other online tools for teaching can innovatively transform learning and student connections, this chapter discusses the destructive use of more casual forms of social media that have found their way into school-based settings.

The Pew Research Center (2015) reported on social media use across America and discovered that as of September 2014, 71 percent of online adults (ages eighteen to sixty-five plus) use Facebook, 23 percent of online adults use Twitter, 26 percent use Instagram, 28 percent use Pinterest, and 28 percent use LinkedIn. Roughly 90 percent of eighteen to twenty-nine year olds have used some type of social-media platform.

Figure 7: Percentage of American Adults and Internet-Using Adults Who Use at Least One Social Networking Site. Social-Media Usage: 2005–2015 (Pew Research Center: Internet, Science and Tech, 2015)

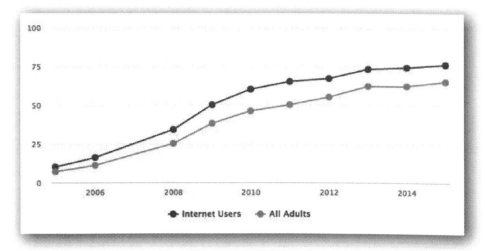

The percentages of those who use social media inappropriately may never be scientifically discovered—as when confronted with their use, many deny using it for unhealthy or destructive reasons. Many individuals, in particular those who work within school settings, morally justify their use of social media. For example, they may say, " I only use Facebook to talk with family members, and I only use Twitter to remind students of homework." Such statements are blatantly false, as these formats offer up opportunities to snoop at others social media platforms and make comments with some belief of anonymity. Frankly, it's no different than someone saying, "I only smoke crack on Wednesday's."

With the use of social-media outlets engrossing the lives of younger-aged students and adults alike, in school environments, the need to associate with a habit that others are engaging in can be a difficult pressure to avoid.

Schools continue to manage students' social-media and cell-phone use with intermittent discipline policies. Very often, schools will state that when social media formats or cell phones are used to bully, intimidate, threaten, or harass other students or school staff, the law does not favor the victim and there is little that can be done to stop the victimizer. Many schools state that cyberbullying is a level of surveillance that is uncontrollable and something that can never be enforced. However, in some specific cases and states across America, the legal authorities may become involved and hold those guilty parties accountable for their violent online behavior.

As a conduit to social media formats, cell phones are now commonly used within school classrooms with teacher discretion, under the guise of a viable instructional method. The hidden truth is that cell phone implementation has been adopted within schools due to previously elevated discipline referrals related to inappropriate student cell phone use. This is another example of how school policy makers use an "If I can't beat them, I'll join them" approach. Cell phone adoption policies have directly contributed to unsanctioned photographs, video footage, cell phone theft, and social media use that are dangerous and non-instructional. In essence, cell phones are now mobile pornographic devices that are school sanctioned. Has there ever been a time in the history of schooling where such a device that is capable of so much has been so freely adopted within school environments without the thought of immediate or long-term harm?

Teacher educators must teach the future teachers of America how to combat inappropriate cell phone usage, social media usage, and cyberbullying among students. Very often the online postings that are made between students or school staff members are inappropriate and become the unseen first round of a future face-to-face altercation. This suppression of aggressive feelings may show themselves in public, long after the harassment began. As it turns out, the remedy for social media use and cyberbullying victimization is remarkably simple.

RETHINKING SOCIAL-MEDIA USE

Social media formats allow people to send pictures, text messages, or video footage of themselves or others, to unlimited numbers of people. What used to be considered private interactions that would be shared in one's home, have now become pictures, text messages, and videos that are shared around the world in a matter of seconds. The invention of specific social media formats has facilitated this ease.

As defined by the American Psychological Association's diagnostic text The *Diagnostic and Statistical Manual of Mental Disorders*, or DSM-5, it's clear that many psychological disorders and behaviors are exuded through the use of social media. The *Diagnostic and Statistical Manual of Mental Disorders* (DSM-5) is the most widely accepted nomenclature used by clinicians and researchers for the classification of mental disorders. For example, with the introduction of the word *selfie* into the mainstream vernacular, such social media practices may give way to narcissism, voyeurism, and exhibitionism, all of which can be psychological disorders. All these words are clearly defined within psychological texts such as DSM-5, or by conducting a simple Google search.

With the definitions of narcissism and vanity being closely linked, they are psychologically defined as; a pervasive pattern of grandiosity (in fantasy or behavior), need for admiration, and lack of empathy, beginning by early adulthood and present in a variety of contexts (APA, 2013). Or, *any erotic gratification derived from admiration of one's own physical or mental attributes, being a normal condition at the infantile level of personality development.* Table 3 below shows characteristics commonly associated with narcissism.

Table 3: Narcissistic Personality Disorder Symptoms (Retrieved from http://psychcentral.com/disorders/narcissistic-personality-disorder-symptoms/)

- Has a grandiose sense of self-importance (exaggerates achievements and talents, expects to be recognized as superior without adequate achievements).
- Is preoccupied with fantasies of unlimited success, power, brilliance, beauty or ideal love.
- Requires excessive admiration from others and strangers.
- Has a very strong sense of entitlement (unreasonable expectations of especially favorable treatment or automatic compliance with his or her expectations).
- Is exploitative of others (takes advantage of others to achieve his or her own ends).
- Lacks empathy.
- Is often envious of others or believes that others are envious of him or her.
- Regularly shows arrogant behaviors or attitudes.
- Believes that he or she is special and unique and can only be understood by or should associate with other special or high-status people (or institutions).

Voyeurism is defined as a paraphilic disorder. This disorder creates sexual gratification on seeing other people perform private activities such as undressing, being naked and/or seeing people performing a sexual act. The target of the person displaying this behavior is aware of the presence of the voyeur, and consents to this behavior. However, in most cases, the voyeur purposefully acts in such a manner without seeking the consent of the target (APA, 2013).

Exhibitionism is commonly characterized as *a tendency to display one's abilities or to behave in such a way as to attract attention.* Exhibitionism is also characterized by *a compulsion to exhibit the genitals in public or to the public.* Examples of this are commonly displayed when individuals take selfies with little or no clothing on, and feel the need to send it to another. While not all forms of exhibitionism are considered disorders, DSM-5 states that the behaviors associated with Exhibitionistic Disorder will occur over a period of six months, are recurrent, and result in intense sexual arousal from the exposure of one's genitals to a stranger or unsuspecting individual (APA, 2013). Ultimately, it's an uncontrollable sexual urge that is deliberately intended for an un-consenting person. Exhibitionistic Disorder results in significant clinical distress and impairs social, occupational, and/or other normal life functions (APA, 2013).

The above behaviors and disorders can be casually displayed over social media outlets. Participants also include younger individuals who feel the need to share self-exposures with their peers or complete strangers. Users, regardless of age or occupation, still believe that these photos or comments are private, even though they can easily be shared or viewed through second or third-hand acquisition (i.e., nonusers viewing another's access to a private account or social-media page, or others taking pictures with their cell phones directly from another's computer screen).

Overall, society refuses to call these acts the psychological conditions they truly are. Nor does society recognize the habits that quickly define them. The mainstream media, and a lack of Internet literacy education are largely to blame for perpetuating this culture among adults and youth. By reporting on these very damaging habits and characterizing them as enjoyable news events, the generated illusion is that such usage and behavior display can bring someone national attention. K–12 classrooms are using social media and cellphones with more regularity as a "viable" classroom instructional method while lacking proper media literacy education beforehand, and throughout. Furthermore, such methods may give way to the early onset of the above conditions and disorders.

Sexting has also become both a new word and a new method of communicating that can easily be tied to the above conditions. Derived from the words *sex* and *texting,* sexting is defined as *the sending of sexually explicit photos, images, text messages or e-mails by using a cell phone or other mobile device.* Sexting can occur among the most immature members of a school, and such photographs can be forced on individuals without their knowledge or consent (i.e., quickly showing a picture to someone with their cell phone). Legally speaking, sexting is a crime when an individual or a group of individuals receive a picture that is unwanted, usually of a nude individual or body part. Plainly speaking, if unwanted, this act is a sex crime regardless of the sender or recipient. Sending someone such pictures when they are unwanted also constitutes the definition of sexual harassment.

If sexting occurs between students both within school environments and away from school, the legal authorities should become involved immediately. If a teacher witnesses the sharing of such photos, that teacher should alert the school's resource officer quickly and quietly. Educators should not let the questioned or guilty party know that they suspect wrongdoing, as the questioned or guilty party may delete the pictures or messages before being investigated. I suggest following up with the school's resource officer to find out what the punishment was for the offence. Make the parents of all parties aware of the behavior in question, even if the school's resource officer fails to do so.

If unwanted sexting occurs in the workplace among staff members, let school administrators know and then get the legal authorities involved. School administrators, in the interest of protecting their professional and public image, may cover up such behaviors. Holding guilty parties accountable with police and legal involvement can send a clear message that such behaviors will not, and should not be tolerated. As stated before, students and adults in school can be no match for the societal pressures placed on them to participate in such unhealthy acts. Philosopher Eric Hoffer stated back in the 1950's that humans would soon become self-advertisers and rely on a need or feeling to self-promote as an illusionary skill, rather than relying on what they know or do not know (Hoffer, 1951). Even back in the 1950's, the self-destructive vain behaviors of today would be predictable.

Ferguson, Muñoz, Garza, and Galindo (2014) stated that exposure to social media, particularly among adolescent girls, may negatively impact body satisfaction, life satisfaction, and eating-disorder symptoms, even though some in the academic community debate these connections. However, Ferguson et al. (2014) stated that peer competition is a larger risk factor and negative habit that is attributed to teenage girls' levels of social media use. The more students use social media, the more they feel the need to compare themselves to their peers (Ferguson et al., 2014). Therefore, peer competition is also exacerbated through social media exposure and use.

By removing themselves from social media outlets and their direct and indirect exposure, individuals may feel less inclined to compare themselves to their peers or overexpose themselves in online formats. Removal from social media outlets can be seen as difficult once use begins, as use can easily become habitual and addictive.

Failure to remove oneself may inflame the associated disorders that come with social media overexposure, such as vanity, body-image problems, self-concept issues, eating disorders, poor self-esteem, anxiety, depression, and suicidal ideation. The risk factors of these destructive social media habits could be taught to K–12 students, school officials, and pre-service teachers at the university level—in an effort to prevent further trauma that impedes student achievement, well-being, and ones overall quality of life.

CYBERBULLYING BEHAVIORS

Hamer den, Konijn, and Keijer (2014) reported that social media use and cyberbullying are cyclical in nature. One aspect of social media use feeds on the participation of another. The authors state that social media content—such as the acts of gossiping, bullying, rough language, and popularization of substance abuse—all contribute to anger and frustration, and lead to participation in acts related to cyberbullying. When a teacher knows of a student who is engaging in social media or cyberbullying, that teacher is more likely to encounter a frustrated and angry student. The same can be true for teachers themselves, as students are not the only ones who engage in social media or cyberbullying. Teachers and administrators can also be willing participants in the misuse of social media communication and cyberbullying. Hamer den et al. (2014) describes the cyclical process of this phenomenon as outlined in figure 8.

Figure 8: A Cyclic Process Model of Cyberbullying Behavior (Hamer den, Konijn, & Keijer, 2014)

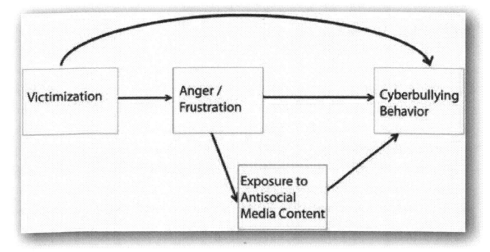

Rice, Petering, Rhoades, Winetrobe, Goldbach, Plant, and Kordic (2015) define cyberbullying as "the repeated use of technology and social media to bully, intimidate or harass, directly or indirectly" (p. 1). Rice et al. (2015) state that cyberbullying is commonly inflicted upon teenage girls who are participating in social media on a regular basis. The authors state that the more people use Facebook, the more likely they are to be the victims of cyberbullying and participate in the very act themselves. Females in particular, who text more than fifty times per day, are also more likely to report online victimization (Rice et al., 2015).

Cyberbullying exists across many platforms. The news media uses Twitter posts from athletes, celebrities, and politicians to highlight their feuds, dissatisfaction, or distaste for one another. While our popular culture has made cyberbullying mainstream, more severe forms are being created regarding the very design of online platforms for hostile communication. For example, a social media phone application titled *After School* (afterschoolapp.com) is designed to have students within schools communicate in anonymous ways, or so one would be led to believe. This online application has lead to the organization of fights, drug deals, and other harmful encounters that have caused serious damage. The very website for this application has teenagers describing how they use it, and the implication is that students can freely hate without reservation or identification. This provides a false sense of anonymity without consequence among participants. Applications of this nature make it evident that our culture has become an opportunistic environment for businesses to profit on the negative behaviors of teenagers. These social media companies pray on students' lack of maturity regarding their patterns of conflict resolution and communication skills, which they need in the real world.

The tragedy and loss of life due to cyberbullying continues to tarnish school districts and the victims' families and loved ones. The lack of education in schools regarding such a psychologically destructive phenomenon is without a doubt a contributor to school violence. Again, K–12 health education curriculum is the only subject matter in school that is responsible for addressing cyberbullying. Hoverer, every educator should lead by example regardless of the class or subject they teach.

The story of Emilie Olsen's life, experiences with cyberbullying, and death; is an example of how schools themselves can be willing participants simply with their failure to act. Emilie Olsen was thirteen years old when she shot herself in the head. She was the victim of cyberbullying and face-to-face bullying within her middle school. The bullying began in elementary school, and her teachers and administrators noted it. When she moved from elementary school to her new middle school, the bullying continued, and again, the administrators, counselor, and teachers were aware of these acts. Given that much of this torment occurred online, many school employees felt there was little they could do. When in fact, there are always steps that can be taken. Below is a video link to watch a description of Emilie's story.

- https://www.youtube.com/watch?v=ukoPUXSr6J8
- YouTube Search Title: *Emilie Olsen: Uncovered evidence shows bullying was factor in 13-year-old's suicide*

When teachers, administrators, or other school employees hear about cyberbullying or any other form of bullying, the steps they should take to eliminate the problem and prevent future acts should be clear. They are the following:

1. Have a school culture that publically addresses the facts surrounding cyberbullying with staff and students and hold it as a zero-tolerance policy.
2. When a complaint arrives, group the suspected students in the same room with one another and discuss any disagreements. Have teachers, parents, and administration present, along with a school resource officer. Record the whole meeting in writing.
3. Demand that the behaviors stop, both online and in person. Encourage all parties to remove themselves from social-media communication platforms.
4. Make sure all parties understand that if the behavior is reported again in any situation, the discipline system will be used to its fullest extent (in-school suspensions, out-of-school suspension, permanent removal from class, reorganization of class schedule, expulsion from the school or district).
5. Make phone calls home to the parents of the students involved and describe what has been reported immediately. Leave voice messages, send e-mails, and record these exchanges in writing.
6. Schedule follow-up conferences with parents and students immediately. Describe to them the problems that have been brought to your attention.

7. If the parents refuse to cooperate or are in denial about their child's behavior, leave voice messages and e-mails reminding them of your duty as a teacher to protect all students.
8. Contact the authorities if you believe a child's life is in danger.
9. Encourage parents to file restraining orders against those guilty of the harassment and bullying.
10. Record every step for the record and keep for future referencing.

If this ten-step process had been followed in the case of Emilie Olsen, she and many others might be alive today. Parents need to talk to their children about the ways they are being treated in school on a daily basis, as the treatment can vary from day to day. Many students refuse to talk to parents or teachers regarding their mistreatment. Many students believe a peaceful resolution will never occur, and that retaliation from victimizers is inevitable if they seek help. These widely held beliefs force students to take the law or the decision-making process into their own hands. For those who are suicidal, complete control over their current situation may result in a tragic ending.

I became involved in defending Emilie Olsen when I found out that she had taken her own life due to bullying in school. I never met Emilie Olsen, nor did I teach in the state where she attended school. However, I did predict that upon her suicide, the school district would refuse to accept responsibility and claim that they knew nothing about the way in which she was being treated. I met with a newspaper reporter for the *Journal-News* in southwest Ohio, close to where Emilie lived and went to school. I discussed with him how bullying information and documentation could easily be erased at the hands of administrators trying to protect their district's public image, as this can be a common practice regarding serious cases. The reporter told me that local police and the district's officials had also intimidated the Olsen family. The school's principal at the time also showed up at the Olsen's house with local police to intimidate the parents into not filing a legal complaint.

I was quoted throughout a follow-up front-page article. Soon after the release of the article, a Cincinnati, Ohio news channel WCPO Channel 9, and an outside investigator, took note of the seriousness of the article and the direct quotations, and conducted a separate investigation. Their inquiry found that the school district willingly hid information that showed that Emilie had been bullied and that the district knew about it, all while doing nothing to stop or prevent further occurrences.

The district superintendent resigned two years after Emilie Olsen's suicide. The principal has also since resigned. The family of Emilie Olsen has brought these issues of negligence to federal court, and they are now suing the school district and the officials directly involved. The charges include: failing to address the bullying, failing to respond to sexual discrimination, failing to respond to race and national origin discrimination, negligence and gross negligence, wrongful death, breach of duty and care of supervision, negligent infliction of emotional distress, hazing and bullying violations, and breach of express or implied contract.

SOCIAL-MEDIA USE AND CYBERBULLYING IN THE WORKPLACE

As stated throughout, students aren't the only guilty parties with regard to violent acts or the inappropriate use of social media. Any human, particularly those who engage in social media platforms, can perpetuate cyberbullying. As a result, Hall and Lewis (2014) stated that cyberbullying and social media use greatly contribute to workplace bullying. What can make the lives of school leaders difficult is when their own employees are engaging in cyberbullying with one another.

Most schools and other workplaces fail to have policies in place to deter such episodes from occurring, or to even properly address consequences if participating adults are caught engaging in these acts. Some schools and school districts have Facebook pages or Twitter accounts that proxy as actual websites. This leads to a method of communication that is solely in the form of Facebook posts or tweets, rather than professional, confidential e-mails. School websites have even adopted instant-messaging formats that encourage teachers to communicate about ideas, to gossip, and to discuss student issues or upcoming events. Such rudimentary forms of communication in professional work settings can invite casual and inappropriate participation. An entire school district may end up viewing a private message that is intended for one individual.

Hall and Lewis (2014) state that because of the overreliance of social media in the workplace as an adopted standard of communication, cyberbullying and e-harassment have become commonplace. These forms of destructive communication plague companies and school districts, while negatively impacting workplace productivity and employee well-being. Hall and Lewis (2014) continue to state that because policies with regard to enforcement of cyberbullying in the workplace and e-harassment are lacking, American employees who are bullied in the workplace might have little recourse, as their bullies are typically promoted and rarely held accountable.

Teachers themselves may boast about their social media use to students in the classroom, and encourage students to participate or communicate with them in the interest of gaining influence. Similar approaches are taken when schoolteachers claim that using social media platforms encourages learning and instruction within classroom settings among their students. This too, is commonly done in an effort to gain superficial influence. Classroom implementation of social media as an instructional method is a dangerous suggestion and one that should be avoided at all costs.

While YouTube and Skype can be facilitated by teachers within classroom settings for positive interaction among students—the use of Facebook, Twitter, Instagram, and other platforms like it should not exist as a part of classroom instruction. Inappropriate use may be likely, and classroom-management nightmares will most certainly become commonplace. True influence is gained not through superficial or materialistic means, but through the personal behaviors of being just, fair, and honest, of possessing common sense, and of being physically, mentally, and emotionally present within the lives of students. Social media instructional methods will never replace the positive influence of human face-to-face emotional authenticity.

It's also been widely recommended that pre-service teachers, current teachers, and administrators remove themselves from social media communication platforms before interviewing for, or holding any educational position. Such a presence on social media platforms can lead school officials to reconsider the hiring of teachers who engage in these forms of communication, or it can quickly lead to their firing. A simple Google web search or Google image search can provide a hiring district or organization all the information they need to make a viable decision.

Root and McKay (2014) reported that prospective teachers and those charged with hiring them have differing opinions on what is considered acceptable social media use. Where a pre-service teacher or current teacher may not view a picture of him or her drinking alcohol, or posing in a bathing suit as inappropriate, many school administrators view such public pictures to be unprofessional, and a major factor in their decision whether or not to hire someone (Root & McKay, 2014).

The most commonly used words on social-media formats are *damn, shit, ass, fuck,* and *bitch* (Griffin & Lake, 2012). Cursing, racist, sexist, or bigoted remarks, suggestive pictures, and other documented forms of association on social media—all influence companies and school leaders in the hiring of employees (Griffin & Lake, 2012). This is why the immediate removal of a current or prospective educator's presence on social media platforms is essential. Not only can such a presence have an impact on the hiring process, but these affiliations can also create the opportunity for bullying. This bullying can come from parents, students, teachers, administrators, and other coworkers, and it can happen without warning.

The acts and habits by those who engage in these forms of online communication have changed the way in which humans communicate with one another. Bala (2014) states that with an overabundance of social media use, the quality of use has diminished considerably. Social media overexposure and overreliance has created a true lack of authenticity in communication and personal development (Bala, 2014). While mass communication has increased because of social media, less virtuous lives are being lived by youth and adults, as communication and interpersonal connections suffer (Bala, 2014). The hype related to social media, as a positive communication platform, is just that: hype (Cardon & Marshall, 2015). The vast majority of business professionals (upward of 89 percent) view traditional face-to-face meetings and over-the-telephone communication as the best way to get things done (Cardon & Marshall, 2015). Many college graduates are having trouble finding teaching positions and other jobs within other organizations due to their online postings or online personas through social media use. This is hindering their ability to apply for jobs, receive interview opportunities, and attain serious career advancements. Therefore realistic media literacy should also exist within undergraduate classes to prepare the future workers of America. Too often, shiny pieces of technology are popularized, particularly within education settings, without a clear examination of the consequences. What some may see as a harmless permanent fixture in our society, may in fact be a dangerous passing fad.

As stated earlier, the remedy is remarkably simple. The most proven way consistently brought up in scholarly research to avoid being victimized on the Internet and social media; is to never become involved in social media and to limit Internet communication. If you choose to communicate over e-mail or social media in the workplace, print off every correspondence for future record. If someone is involved in social media and becomes victimized, removing oneself from visual, verbal, and habitual participation is the quickest solution.

As it turns out, many who quit and permanently stop using Facebook, Twitter, Instagram, Pinterest, and LinkedIn, tend to report similar reflective feelings associated with this lifestyle change. These revelations are also shared among those who stop abusing drugs and alcohol or those who permanently give up any addictive habit. These feelings include, but are not limited to the following:

- Having more time to commit to more important things
- Possessing stronger, more meaningful relationships
- Focusing on work or personal time in a more productive manner
- Freeing up time to think about future goals
- Feeling less selfish and self-absorbed
- Ultimately wondering what they could have been doing with their time had they not participated in these habits
- Feeling regret for past misuse or overuse

SUMMARY POINTS FOR CHAPTER 4

- Teacher educators must teach the future teachers of America how to combat inappropriate social media use and cyberbullying among their students.
- Exhibitionism, voyeurism, and narcissism are all psychological disorders that by definition are associated with social media use.
- If sexting occurs between students within school, away from school, and is unwanted, the legal authorities should become involved immediately.
- Peer competition is a large risk factor and a negative habit that is attributed to teenage girls' levels of social media use. The higher the social-media use, the more students feel the need to compare themselves to their peers.
- Social media use may inflame vanity, body-image and self-concept issues, eating disorders, poor self-esteem, anxiety, depression, and suicide.

- Cell-phone use in the classroom, instructional or otherwise, should not be allowed.
- The ten-step process proposed for addressing improper social media use and cyberbullying among students in school should be considered.
- Cyberbullying and social media use greatly contributes to workplace bullying.
- Cursing, racist, sexist or bigoted remarks, suggestive pictures, and other documented forms of association on social media all influence companies and school leaders in the hiring of employees.
- The majority of business professionals view traditional face-to-face meetings and telephone verbal communication as the best way to get things done.

5

School-Related Suicide

Before the thoughts of suicide enter one's mind, an individual must already be suffering from depression or possess the associated symptoms of such a condition. Rarely does a healthy-minded person wake up and decide that today is the day to end his or her own life, or even attempt to do so. The onset of poor mental health and prolonged unchecked mental health, can lead to such thoughts, which may result in a permanent physical action.

While this chapter focuses on the factors that impact school-aged students, teachers and school staff members also attempt and complete suicide. *Completing suicide* is a term that is used when someone is successful in his or her own suicide attempt to the point of completion or death. School staff and students can attempt or complete suicide for very similar reasons. As mentioned in chapter 2, teacher burnout and work-related stressors are major factors that impact a mental and emotional decline that can lead to the actions related to suicide. As described later in chapter 10, workplace bullying is also a major contributing factor to suicide ideation among school staff. Technically speaking, every chapter within this book describes the factors that lead to such destructive personal thoughts or actions.

As previously mentioned, environmental factors such as family, school, relationships, academic achievement, and acceptance levels; largely contribute to the decline of personal well-being. When students kill themselves in school or leave notes describing why they took their own life and they blame the school, when does the school take the responsibility? Perhaps the structures of schools, the cliques, clubs, traditions, lack of appropriate discipline, and adult unreliability—can be too much for a teenager or teacher to handle.

TEENAGE SUICIDE

On May 14, 2015, eighteen-year-old Marcus Wheeler shot himself in school in front of many witnesses, including the female resource officer who attempted to stop him.

Marcus attended Corona Del Sol High School in Tempe, Arizona. The news report on his death spent time discussing that as he was a star on the cross-country team, a senior set to graduate, and that such an act was "absolutely unthinkable." Local media interviewed parents of other students within the same school, but they only discussed how they couldn't imagine why teenagers kill themselves in school.

Such acts of personal violence always have a cause. They aren't unthinkable. When a student takes his or her own life, particularly at school, the finger may point directly at the school and the people within as potentially assisting in the mental and emotional breakdown of that student. Sadly, school officials are rarely if ever blamed, and they almost always publically state that they never saw such an act of violence coming, and that there would be no way to predict such an episode in the future. This "sweeping the dirt under the rug" approach perpetuates the problem. Schools can make kids sick. More people should investigate and monitor how peers, teachers, coaches, and school leaders are treating students attending their school. The truthful reasons behind a student's suicide may ultimately be covered up. The true reasons for the suicide of Marcus Wheeler, and many like him, may never be fully known.

The CDC's division of violence prevention (CDC, 2015) reports that among youth between the ages of ten and twenty-four, suicide is the second and third leading cause of death. This adds up to around four thousand, six hundred deaths each year. The top forms of suicide among youth include firearm (45 percent), suffocation (40 percent), and poisoning (8 percent). Suicide by firearms is self-explanatory. Suicide by suffocation however, can include intentional or unintentional death, such as huffing (the inhaling of poisonous substances) and deaths attributed to hanging or self-strangulation. Suicide by poisoning may be related to accidently or intentionally overdosing on drugs and or alcohol.

Many deaths among school-aged students are attributed to accidents. Unintentional injury is the number-one cause of death among this age group, and most other age groups. However, it becomes difficult for anyone to know the true motives behind such deaths attributed to suicide, particularly if the school environment is to blame. This may be another reason why students complete suicide in school, before school, or immediately after school. Students may want to leave little doubt as to who or what contributed to their declining frame of mind. Some people may also state that school shootings or school-related stabbings are another form of suicide. It's very common for those victimizers to fully understand that they are not going to get away with their violent behavior. Therefore, its widely know that their actions will lead to their suicide or their death at the hands of responding law enforcement officials.

Table 4: Ten Leading Causes of Death by Age Group—US (CDC, 2013)

10 Leading Causes of Death by Age Group, United States - 2013

Rank	<1	1-4	5-9	10-14	15-24	25-34	35-44	45-54	55-64	65+	Total
1	Congenital Anomalies 4,758	Unintentional Injury 1,316	Unintentional Injury 745	Unintentional Injury 775	Unintentional Injury 11,619	Unintentional Injury 16,209	Unintentional Injury 15,354	Malignant Neoplasms 46,185	Malignant Neoplasms 113,324	Heart Disease 488,156	Heart Disease 611,105
2	Short Gestation 4,202	Congenital Anomalies 476	Malignant Neoplasms 447	Malignant Neoplasms 448	Suicide 4,878	Suicide 6,348	Malignant Neoplasms 11,349	Heart Disease 35,167	Heart Disease 72,568	Malignant Neoplasms 407,558	Malignant Neoplasms 584,881
3	Maternal Pregnancy Comp. 1,595	Homicide 337	Congenital Anomalies 179	Suicide 386	Homicide 4,329	Homicide 4,236	Heart Disease 10,341	Unintentional Injury 20,357	Unintentional Injury 17,057	Chronic Low. Respiratory Disease 127,194	Chronic Low. Respiratory Disease 149,205
4	SIDS 1,563	Malignant Neoplasms 328	Homicide 125	Congenital Anomalies 161	Malignant Neoplasms 1,496	Malignant Neoplasms 3,673	Suicide 6,551	Liver Disease 8,785	Chronic Low. Respiratory Disease 17,942	Cerebro-vascular 109,602	Unintentional Injury 130,557
5	Unintentional Injury 1,156	Heart Disease 169	Chronic Low. Respiratory Disease 75	Homicide 152	Heart Disease 941	Heart Disease 3,258	Homicide 2,581	Suicide 8,621	Diabetes Mellitus 15,942	Alzheimer's Disease 84,767	Cerebro-vascular 128,978
6	Placenta Cord Membranes 953	Influenza & Pneumonia 102	Influenza & Pneumonia 73	Heart Disease 100	Congenital Anomalies 362	Diabetes Mellitus 684	Liver Disease 2,491	Diabetes Mellitus 5,899	Liver Disease 13,061	Diabetes Mellitus 53,751	Alzheimer's Disease 84,767
7	Bacterial Sepsis 578	Chronic Low. Respiratory Disease 64	Heart Disease 67	Chronic Low. Respiratory Disease 80	Influenza & Pneumonia 197	Liver Disease 676	Diabetes Mellitus 1,952	Cerebro-vascular 5,425	Cerebro-vascular 11,364	Influenza & Pneumonia 48,031	Diabetes Mellitus 75,578
8	Respiratory Distress 522	Septicemia 53	Cerebro-vascular 41	Influenza & Pneumonia 61	Diabetes Mellitus 193	HIV 631	Cerebro-vascular 1,687	Chronic Low. Respiratory Disease 4,619	Suicide 7,135	Unintentional Injury 45,942	Influenza & Pneumonia 56,979
9	Circulatory System Disease 458	Benign Neoplasms 47	Benign Neoplasms 35	Cerebro-vascular 48	Complicated Pregnancy 178	Cerebro-vascular 508	HIV 1,246	Septicemia 2,445	Septicemia 5,345	Nephritis 39,080	Nephritis 47,112
10	Neonatal Hemorrhage 389	Perinatal Period 45	Benign Neoplasms 34	Benign Neoplasms 31	Chronic Low. Respiratory Disease 155	Influenza & Pneumonia 449	Influenza & Pneumonia 881	HIV 2,378	Nephritis 4,947	Septicemia 28,815	Suicide 41,149

Age Groups

Data Source: National Vital Statistics System, National Center for Health Statistics, CDC.
Produced by: National Center for Injury Prevention and Control, CDC using WISQARS™.

Centers for Disease Control and Prevention
National Center for Injury Prevention and Control

A much larger statistic is the amount of attempts an individual will take to end his or her own life. The CDC's division of violence prevention (CDC, 2015) states that each year, approximately one hundred and fifty-seven thousand youths, between the ages of ten and twenty-four, receive medical treatment for self-inflicted injuries at emergency departments across America. This should alarm school leaders into action. Abusing alcohol, taking illegal drugs, smoking, being sexually promiscuous, and even driving too fast, are common habits among students in school that could easily be interoperated as forms of self-harming. In essence, school officials largely see the contributing factors to teen suicide, yet they may fail to make the comparison from one destructive habit to the final act of a depression-related illness.

The CDC's division of violence prevention page (CDC, 2015) even admits the negligence and lack of awareness surrounding such preventative education. The web page states, "Most people are uncomfortable with the topic of suicide. Too often, victims are blamed, and their families and friends are left stigmatized. As a result, people do not communicate openly about suicide. Thus, an important public health problem is left shrouded in secrecy, which limits the amount of information available to those working to prevent suicide." The quantity and quality of information on this topic is not lacking. There is no logical excuse for failing to teach the preventive measures and long-term impacts of suicide, particularly among school-aged students.

SUICIDE AMONG STUDENT ATHLETES

High-school sports now air daily on ESPN and other sports channels. American towns and cities place an immense emphasis on student participation in school-related sports. Sadly, it's commonly assumed that if students play school sanctioned sports, then they become immune to judgments, negative emotions, or mental disorders that can lead to depressive thoughts or suicidal ideation. With the never-ending trend of sports in school and the widely adopted phrase *student athlete*, there may be a rise in creating a culture of entitlement, secrecy, distraction, and neglect. These characteristics can give rise to the behaviors commonly associated with suicidal ideation.

Yang, Peek-Asa, Corlette, Cheng, Foster, and Albright (2007) conducted a survey of 257 collegiate student athletes (167 males and ninety females) who participated in Division I National Collegiate Athletic Association (NCAA) sponsored sports, during the 2005–2006 school year. Symptoms of depression were measured as were symptoms of anxiety and other health-related risk factors, using widely adopted medical measurements.

The results of the surveys concluded that 21 percent of those surveyed reported experiencing symptoms of depression. Athletes who were freshmen with self-reported physical pain were more likely to experience symptoms of depression. Female athletes in particular, had greater odds of experiencing symptoms of depression compared to male student athletes. Freshmen also had also greater odds of experiencing symptoms of depression than their senior peers. Student athletes who reported symptoms of depression were also associated with higher rates of anxiety.

Even though this study was conducted among college student athletes, the risk factors for depression and the potential for thoughts of suicide may be the same among middle and high school students who play one sport or multiple sports. It could be stated that the levels of competition, the risk to injury, and the fear of failure to achieve what was expected or demanded of them, can all play a role in the mental and emotional decline of student athletes.

SUICIDE AMONG TALENTED AND GIFTED STUDENTS

It's also widely assumed that students who excel academically are healthier and have a heightened sense of well-being. Truthfully, this is an incorrect assumption. Students who excel academically may have a backstory that is inundated with personal and parental pressure, high expectations, a divisive competitive nature, and a "win at all cost" mentality. The teachers of these students can also place an inordinate amount of unrealistic pressure on them. Ultimately, disappointment may affect these students more readily than those who might otherwise be considered average students.

Dr. Tracy Cross examines teen suicide among talented and gifted students in his book *Suicide Among Gifted Children and Adolescents: Understanding The Suicidal Mind.* In this very important book, Dr. Cross states that most teachers are able to quickly identify students in danger. However, among those students who excel academically, it's often overlooked, seen as nonexistent, or viewed as a temporary problem by their teachers. When in fact, these very students may be the most likely to have depressive thoughts due to the pressures to achieve, and other related factors that give way to depression, suicidal ideation, and suicide completion (Cross, 2013).

According to Dr. Cross, suicide-identification and prevention measures should be taught to teachers and students of all ages in an attempt to stem the tide of such negative thoughts or actions. Educators and schools placing high or unrealistic amounts of pressure on their students can lead to deadly effects well into college (Cross, 2013). It's worth keeping in mind that suicide is the second-leading cause of death among college students (CDC, 2013). Cross (2013) also states that counseling for talented and gifted students may be vital. This approach may come with a social stigma, or not be relied upon due to a lack of visible factors. However, checking for the levels of well-being among these students may be a preventive measure that school officials and parents should consider.

Cassady and Cross (2006) examined a range of suicidal thoughts among students enrolled in a talented and gifted public school. Their study looked at suicidal ideation among academically gifted adolescents. The results of the questionnaire given to students revealed that cognitive, environmental, and psychological factors were highly present during the first of four factors: *suicidal pragmatics, morbid fixation, social isolation,* and *social impact.* The frequency of entertaining the thought of suicide among gifted students was also much higher among the pragmatic factor, than other factors (Cassady & Cross, 2006). In summary, the vast majority of the students surveyed believed that suicide was the most reasonable way to solve their problems if faced with serious obstacles.

Abbott and Zakriski (2014) discussed how adolescent suicide impacts those teenagers who are personally connected to those who intentionally end their own lives. The results of their study showed that the closer a person personally was to a peer who completed suicide, the higher the level of grief that person felt. This same group also believed that suicide was not preventable in nature. The second group questioned was made up of those who were not previously associated with a suicide cluster or peer-associated suicide. This group described suicide as more normal, yet incomprehensible (Abbott & Zakriski, 2014).

The hypothesis made by the authors was that the closer one is to a peer who completes suicide, the more grief one will experience and the less stigmatizing beliefs that person will have. As it turned out, this was not true. Grief was widespread among all groups, including those exposed to peer suicide and those not exposed to suicide. Peer support, family support, and education seemed to help with the beliefs regarding suicide and the causes of its occurrence. However, students surveyed stated that failed preventive measures for suicide both created and added to a sense of hopelessness (Abbott & Zakriski, 2014). Addressing the need for preventive education, while not stigmatizing suicide (calling them sinners or weak minded), may have a positive impact on both the students in school and the frequency of communication regarding the ideation of suicidal thoughts.

SUICIDE AND CYBERBULLYING

With forms of traditional face-to-face and behind-the-back bullying being common within school environments, cyberbullying has taken shape over the last decade as a major cause of peer-directed aggression and individualized self-aggression. I want to examine how cyberbullying plays a role in increased suicidal ideation.

Cyberbullying is defined by Hinduja and Patchin (2010) as the willful and repeated harm inflicted on others through electronic devices, such as cell phones, computers, and other forms of communication. In essence, it's the same definition as traditional bullying and harassment. Cyberbullying is anonymous, or personally identified repetitious harassment over an electronic device, typically viewed by a single person or a larger audience. It's been estimated that almost a quarter of students who engage in online communication have been cyberbullied. It should come as no surprise that this form of harassment has a negative mental and emotional impact on those who engage in such habits.

Hinduja and Patchin (2010) surveyed over one thousand middle school students regarding their experiences with cyberbullying, and discovered that both victims and victimizers reported increased thoughts of suicide. While students reported engaging in cyberbullying specifically related to posting something online to make fun of someone and make others laugh (23.1 percent), more students engaged in face-to-face or traditional bullying in the same way (27.7 percent). Hinduja and Patchin (2010) described that there is a slight distinction between offending someone online and victimizing them (offensive behavior is not necessarily repetitious, while victimization requires repetition).

In relation to these two behaviors, victimization was reported to have a longer and more consequential impact with regard to suicidal ideation. Hinduja and Patchin (2010) discovered that suicidal ideation was also dependent on race. In their study, nonwhites reported thoughts of suicide more often than whites. This goes against some national statistics that state that whites are more often suicidal. However, this researched information by Hinduja and Patchin (2010) may be dependent on other factors within a school environment, such as being in the minority of a school's demographics (sex, race, or ethnicity), being isolated, feeling singled out, feeling left out, being ridiculed, or being put down.

Many research articles tend to respond in the same way about how cyberbullying can be prevented or even stopped. The answer they give is—*stay off the Internet's social media sites*. It's that simple. If a person is not around the very thing that is causing the harm, then that person is less likely to be negatively impacted by it. The same could be stated about suicidal ideation and surrounding oneself with peers who consistently talk about such behaviors. All students, regardless of categorical makeup, may consider the Internet and the associated forms of communication as a "safe place" where they can express themselves freely. However, it can be within these same online environments where they are victimized, thereby making their false online environment no different than their real one.

Research still calls for educators and school leaders to address these issues that cause suicidal ideation, such as cyberbullying, to be taught within health education curriculum. This may be the only class that is required to address such serious issues impacting students. A lack of realistic media literacy also exists within college classes at the undergraduate level. Such a lack of realistic preventative education may be compounding the issue of suicide as the second-leading cause of death among college students (CDC, 2013). Media literacy, combined with ones immediate removal from social media outlets, may be the best-case scenario. Otherwise, the factors related to depression and the illnesses that lead to suicide, may go largely ignored. These habits may be perpetuated due to a simple lack of understating.

Clearly there is a need for school leaders, teachers of current students, and those training to be teachers, to immerse themselves in the necessary education and literature, in order to deter suicidal ideation among all students. Teachers, students, and school administrators must be certain that they are not adding to the aggressive thoughts that may give way to depression, self-harm, or the completion of suicide among students. The more one reads about the statistical facts related to childhood and adolescent suicide and compares them to scientific research, the more one may see the connections between neglectful school environments and a lack of addressing the mental and emotional needs of all students.

A lack of a health education and suicide prevention curriculum being taught to elementary, middle, and high school students may also add to this problem. Sadly, schools typically rely on quick fixes and one-time guest speakers to address such serious issues. A suicide prevention curriculum that is taught by qualified and certified individuals who work within the school full-time (i.e., health education teachers) accompanied by realistic professional development for school staff, may be the most impactful solution.

SUMMARY POINTS FOR CHAPTER 5

- The CDC reports that for youths between the ages of ten and twenty-four, suicide is the third-leading cause of death. This adds up to around four thousand six hundred deaths each year. The top forms of suicide among youth include firearms (45 percent), suffocation (40 percent), and poisoning (8 percent).
- Such acts of personal violence always have a cause. They aren't unthinkable. Students taking their own lives, particularly at school, may directly point the finger at the school as potentially assisting in the mental and emotional breakdown of students.
- The CDC states that each year approximately one hundred fifty-seven thousand youths between the ages of ten and twenty-four receive medical treatment for self-inflicted injuries at emergency departments across America.
- Abusing alcohol, taking illegal drugs, being sexually promiscuous, and even driving too fast are common habits among students in school that could easily be interpreted as forms of self-harming.
- The failure to remove school-based pressures having little effect on the long-term well-being of students may be largely to blame for a rapid decline in the mental and emotional health of students. The presence of such clubs, groups, and school pressures may lead students to completing suicide.
- College athletes report experiencing symptoms of depression. In particular, freshman and female athletes have greater odds of experiencing symptoms of depression compared to male student athletes.

- Teachers can quickly identify students in peril; however, among those students who excel academically, suicide is often overlooked as nonexistent or a temporary problem. Talented and gifted students should also receive counseling throughout such rigid academic programs.
- Talented and gifted students can view suicide and suicidal ideation as a practical way of solving problems.
- Among students who were the victims of cyberbullying and those who were the victimizers, both parties reported increased thoughts of suicide.
- Teachers and school leaders should discuss with students their interests in keeping a safe environment for all.
- Educators should learn to recognize the warning signs of suicide and immediately address them with students and should gain assistance from a school counselor if a student is suspected of having these thoughts or shares them.

6

The Dynamics of Physical Violence in School

The most common forms of physical violence a student is likely to experience typically involve physical contact between two parties directly. Fistfights, stabbings, school shootings, bomb threats, and other physical crimes do occur. But, the daily physical torment between students can be just as damaging, and they may ultimately lead to mass killings and other destructive conclusions.

Jan and Husain (2015) stated in their study regarding the causes of bullying in elementary schools, that "power achievement" and "physical violence" are the two most common reasons for both bullying and physical violence among students. Those who engage in these acts of physical aggression are also likely to be victims of these behaviors themselves (Jan & Husain, 2015). However, these two reasons are not singular to elementary schools. For example, the circumstances surrounding the student shooters within Columbine High School on April 29, 1999 in Littleton, Colorado may not have been truthfully explained to the public. This school shooting left thirteen dead and twenty-one injured and it's commonly the most discussed example of a K–12 public school shootings. However, the true facts are not widely shared. The local and national media would rather paint another picture in the wake of such an episode, and they did so in this situation.

On an ABC News program titled *The Day It Happened: The Columbine Shootings*, ABC News's Charlie Gibson interviews three students who witnessed the day of the shooting. Perhaps the most telling reasons for the school shooting are uncovered during this very interview. Charlie Gibson interviews Krystal, a junior; Josh, a sophomore; and Justin, a freshman. All three students briefly discussed their participation within the school's sports programs. Charlie Gibson himself says, "This is the group the shooters were directly targeting, yes?" The three interviewed students responded, "Yes." Josh said, that the shooters entered the library and told everyone, "All of the jocks please stand up! If anyone has a hat on or sports emblem on them, you're dead!" Josh then said, "It looked like they were picking people out. They appeared to be picking people out who were jocks, or of that sort. If they saw their friend they would let them go."

Throughout this very short, yet very revealing interview, the interviewed students themselves place the blame and the motives behind the shooting directly on the school staff. The students and school staff throughout the entire school knew who these shooters were, and they knew of their reputations and previous behaviors. These student shooters had a history of being bullied by both students and school staff, publically. Charlie Gibson even asked, "Is this group, this Trench Coat Mafia, were they very well know around the school? When you see them around school wearing these trench coats walking around the school, what kind of aura did they have?" The students responded by saying, "They were always mad...everyone knew who they were... and now the pieces all make sense." Charlie Gibson concludes the program by quickly stating that the investigators assigned to the school shooting believe that "The motives remain a mystery. There are no specific clues, but teachers and students should watch out for any disturbing behavior."

The motives aren't a mystery, and there were very obvious clues dating back months before this school shooting. The students and school staff had directly and indirectly bullied these student shooters repeatedly before the school shooting.

Family members of the school shooters were partially blamed. Gun control was blamed. Politicians were blamed, and musicians were blamed. Soon after the Columbine shooting in 1999, schools across America disallowed trench coats and long heavy winter coats in response, and such coats were now labeled a dress-code violation. Students who wore these coats were frequently suspended from school. Some students even had their coats confiscated permanently. School administrators routinely told students to simply buy new coats. Yes, that's right—coats were also blamed.

At no point were the teachers, administrators, parents, or students within Columbine High School blamed for perpetuating or failing to prevent this deadly physical act. Perhaps what is just as disturbing, is that the ABC News program with Charlie Gibson and the interview with the three student witnesses, is impossible to find. I recorded this program directly from the Apple iTunes store when it originally aired on television sometime around 2007. A copy of this television program and the students' interview no longer exist. It has been completely removed from the Internet, including the Apple iTunes store, Google, and YouTube.

GROUP DYNAMICS OF PHYSICAL VIOLENCE

In his collection of essays regarding human obedience (*The Individual in a Social World*), Stanley Milgram (1992) discusses the actions of individuals specifically within urban communities who witness crimes. Given the geographical and environmental makeup of such a community, particularly when there are large numbers of individuals living in close proximity to one another, when a crime occurs—the vast majority of citizens refuse to become involved in catching the criminal or even providing truthful information that may lead to an arrest.

Dr. Milgram states that this phenomenon occurs, in large part, due to a refusal to adjust present social norms. If criminal behavior is an expectation or norm within a group or organization, one's further involvement in solving the problem may disrupt that preexisting norm. A lack of intervention can also exist due to a perceived threat of harm by association. This mindset provides us with the origin of the words *snitching* and *ratting*. Dr. Milgram discovered that this reluctance to solve problems also leads to rudeness, neglect, rumor spreading, group peer pressure, and a feeling of anonymity.

An individual may desperately seek to belong to a group even if that belonging is harmful. Schools are not free from this proven research. As stated earlier, these very characteristics could easily characterize school environments, as the truth is rarely reported in its entirety when it comes to daily violent acts of a physical nature. This is particularly true if the social norm is to reduce occurrences of physical violence while minimizing the reporting of such episodes.

In another famous observational study by Dr. Milgram, a single pedestrian was asked to stand on a New York City sidewalk at a dead stop, and look in an upward direction. This was done to test if others would also stop and look up, even though the pedestrian was not looking at anything in particular. This took place over the course of two days, and pictures were taken across the street in an adjacent building to measure the size and frequency of movement among the group. As each hour passed, more and more pedestrians stopped and looked in the direction of where the single pedestrian was standing and looking. This proved that regardless of what was occurring or whether it had any meaning, individuals hold a strong curiosity about where others are and where they are looking, along with a desire to participate in similar activities. These beliefs can dominate behavior, particularly when the crowd size increases. This also shows how the actions and behaviors of one—can easily influence the actions and behaviors of many.

This research is also relevant when compared to physical fights within schools. The majorities of students stop, turn, stare, freeze, or even create a circle pattern around the volatile parties or the noticed disruption. This typically occurs when one of the students' peers is engaging in an act that is unknown, uncomfortable or violent. Recognizing these group formations from a distance is a skill a teacher needs to acquire in order to intervene and prevent harmful acts. This can be accomplished with a teacher's presence in or around the group in question, thereby preventing its very formation. A teacher's diligent presence as students travel in groups can be a pronounced preventive method.

One example of this behavior, that is all too common in school environments, occurs at the very beginning of a school day. As students walk into a school, too often they are allowed by a schools administration to gather in groups, typically in open areas, instead of immediate classroom attendance upon entry being the expectation. Within these settings, the group dynamic typically takes on circle formations where students can see one another. Such formations are common when individuals want to seek attention, or feel direct or indirect connections with their peers. Students may even go so far as to squeeze in between people, thus making physical contact with those around them. This is done in an effort to feel more associated with the conversation or with the person or persons leading the group. This behavior can also be witnessed among crowds at musical concerts. In order to feel closer to the experience, audience members abandon any personal anxiety regarding physical contact with strangers. They may even shove, bump, punch, or yell at one another to simply get closer or feel more connected.

The physical design of school hallways can also create boundary issues that are likely to lead to an increase in physical violence. Given that school hallways are typically narrow, the odds of students bumping into one another are remarkably high. To remedy this age-old habit, perhaps schools should let students leave class based on the time on the clock rather than on a bell ringing. This very practice occurs within college and university settings when a class has reached its conclusion. Younger, less mature children and adolescents in school may also benefit from extra time in order to avoid or maneuver through a crowd.

Depending on the school, rules may also require students to walk on designated sides of the hallway or to follow a particular line to avoid running into one another. Below are examples of typical hallways in school settings that may lead to an increase or decrease in physical contact.

Figure 9: Elementary School Hallway with Directional Lines and No Lockers

Figure 10: Middle School/High School Hallway with Lockers on Top of and Across from One Another /No Lines

The architecture of schools is changing as a result of this knowledge about proximity and physical contact among students. More and more schools are being built without lockers on top of one another, and some engineers of schools are even removing the presence of lockers altogether. Larger hallways are also being designed for space issues and security purposes. As schools take these design considerations into account, the security of the students and the school staff should consistently be at the forefront. However, many schools fail to make these engineering accommodations.

Congregating group dynamics occur within school settings typically with the compliance of school officials. It should be no surprise that physical violence is likely to occur within these group formations at the beginnings and ends of school days. I would equate it to handing a toddler a full glass of water without a lid on it. But instead of handing the glass of water directly to the toddler, you set it on the edge of a high table just within the toddler's reach, and then you back away. The act that follows is inevitable, and schools themselves may set up these very risky group dynamics, thereby increasing the chances of student physical contact and the potential for a violent act. The linking of one risk factor with another, repeatedly, is commonly referred to as *cumulative risk*.

Regardless of the current or new designs of schools, daily and persistent supervision of students by teachers, administrators, and school resource officers is crucial. If the student groups become too big—thereby setting the stage for physical contact, violence, or aggression—a redesign or removal of environmental elements and group dynamics must take place.

PHYSICAL VIOLENCE AMONG STUDENTS OFF SCHOOL GROUNDS

As stated earlier, failure to intervene and prevent these actions appropriately may result in work-related reprimands and legal liability. But what happens when such displays of physical violence are perpetuated among school-aged students out of the sight or presence of school employees? How do schools react to such cases that take place away from school grounds? In the case of Naomi Johnson, the answer is that no one helps.

Naomi Johnson was a high-school student in Anchorage, Alaska, when her "friends" invited her over to their house for a sleepover. When she entered her friend's house, over half-a-dozen girls and a few boys physically assaulted her, recorded it with a phone, and posted it on the Internet. I encourage everyone to read this article about the assault and watch the video that was taken by her assailants, and then posted online. The film and article are located at the following web address and the film is graphic in nature.

- http://www.thedailybeast.com/articles/2015/12/14/teens-upload-brutal-video-of-sleepover-attack.html
- https://www.youtube.com/watch?v=O6MhrwJDuCI
- YouTube Search Title: *A Bullying Nightmare*

As the first video explains, given that the children were all underage, criminal charges were slow to proceed, and ultimately no charges were filled. The school's administration offered their opinion and stated that there was little they could do given that the assault occurred off school grounds. Sadly this is where schools decide to practice

60

discretion. The school's administration even stated that they "care about the well-being of all of their students."

When schools fail to act, even in issues away from school grounds, when their own students are involved, they directly and indirectly send a message to every teacher, student, and the community—that safety and well-being do not come first. In the case of Naomi's attackers, at the very least all the identified attacking students should have been expelled by the school district. Criminal charges should have been filed quickly by city authorities for assault and battery, if not attempted murder.

Schools may state that student accountability is difficult when violent acts occur off school grounds between students. This is untrue. Schools typically don't have policies on record that describe such involvement one way or another. However, by documenting the rules and regulations for the potential of such circumstances, school districts would be taking a necessary preventive measure. Such a step may discourage students from associating with those who engage is such violent acts, or the very act itself may ultimately be prevented.

PHYSICAL DATING VIOLENCE

Dating relationships are common among school-aged students. While many of these relationships are immature and superficial, such relationships typically begin around the middle- and high-school years. Given students' lack of knowledge about dating relationships, students tend to rely on personal feelings, peer influence, and past or current environmental exposure regarding how to behave.

Students who engage in dating relationships at young ages tend to be at risk for lower rates of school success and poorer mental and emotional maturity. Nahapetyan, Orpinas, Song, and Holland (2014) state that among those who engage in dating relationships within high school (grades nine through twelve), one-forth of students reported thoughts of suicide by the time they were in twelfth grade, while approximately half of students in dating relationships reported physical violence within those relationships. Nahapetyan et al. (2014) also reported in their study that teenagers who reported physical violence within their relationships were twice as likely to report thoughts of suicide. Given the maturation level of the individuals engaging in these dating relationships, such responses may shine a light on the need for more education through health-education classes in order to address the statistical facts regarding teenage dating.

Engaging in intimate relationships at early ages has shown over time to negatively impact future relationships and academic success, while heightening the risks of sexual promiscuity, drug use, physical aggression, and other negative health-related factors. Without a proper education or positive examples, both in school and within the home, students may easily give in to the pressures to date before they are mentally and emotionally mature enough to deal with the consequences. Teachers should pay attention to these risk factors and become familiar with their students who are engaging in dating relationships by simply observing.

By paying attention from a distance, a teacher can intervene when a behavior is inappropriate, even though the teenager may not see it as such. Excessive touching, public displays of affection (PDA), pulling of the arms, waist, or hair; groping, and the presence of visible bruising, red marks, and handprints (on the neck, arms, legs or face) can all be seen by an observant teacher. These behaviors should be discouraged and stopped immediately, and then the safer behaviors should be taught. The teacher should address this with the offending parties, their parents, and the other school officials. Parent conferences for such behaviors may shine a light on other behaviors or personal feelings toward such relationships. Parents always have the right to know what is happening to their child or how their child is behaving in school, even in dating relationships.

By correcting negative dating relationship behaviors among students, teachers and administrators can have a positive influence on the direction of those associations. Teachers and administrators should not ignore students' dating relationships or the potential signs of dating violence. Safety and security are still a teacher's number one responsibility, even in a student's dating relationship when it can be observed throughout the school environment.

PHYSICAL VIOLENCE BY AND TOWARD SCHOOL STAFF

As a result of aggression, miscommunication, poor communication, unprofessionalism, or a surplus of other factors, violent acts within schools can be perpetuated by school staff toward students, and by students toward school staff. If ideological or authoritarian differences are present—and they tend to be—the aggression levels of both school staff and students can intensify.

While these forms of violence are not highly publicized, they may be the most heinous. While acts such as this can occur in the shadows of a school environment on a daily basis, other acts of violence between these parties can occur with many witnesses, and they can be caught on film with cell phones or security cameras, then quickly uploaded online. As the video below describes, a teacher became frustrated with a student's bullying behavior and organized a physical assault on the student with the help of older students within the same school.

- https://www.youtube.com/watch?v=Miu_10h7vSo
- YouTube Search Title: *Did Florida teacher order a hit on student?*

While this type of behavior may seem rare, unreported cases of violent behavior toward students at the hands of teachers or administrators may go largely unreported or hidden from the public eye. Teachers pushing, shoving, verbally threatening, or throwing objects at students, can be commonplace in unprofessional school cultures. In each case, students should report these incidents in writing and in person to the school's administration and proper authority figures. Even if they themselves are not the direct victims but have observed the behavior, witnessing students still have a responsibly to report such heinous acts.

School violence directed toward staff members by students also poses a threat to the safety of the working environment. Specifically, yet largely unreported and very common, is the frequency of teachers and administrators avoiding engagement with students who have a reputation of physical aggression, verbal aggression, or violent behavior. In particular, when there are many witnesses to such behaviors. For example, teachers and administrators may be less likely to confront aggressive students, particularly if the students are a different race, gender, or size than the witnessing teacher or administrator. Any feelings that add to an already existing discomfort, can lead to negligence of a school staff member's professional responsibilities. This absence or fear of intervening can perpetuate the aggressive student's destructive behavior. Intervening each and every time regardless of a student's size, race, gender, or previous history of violence, is essential. Teachers and administrators should never ignore such behavior and the immediate recruitment of fellow staff members may help alleviate any anxiety in addressing these aggressive students alone or directly.

In their article titled *Physical Assault of School Personnel*, Kajs, Schumacher, and Vital (2014) highlighted case studies and specific episodes of violence toward teachers, by students. In one highlighted example, a student slaps a teacher for getting too close to them when the teacher asks the student to finish their schoolwork. The student rips up their own papers and slaps the teacher across the face, causing swelling and a laceration. The teacher immediately leaves school and goes to the hospital. While at the hospital, the teacher calls the police to report the incident and file criminal charges. The school's administration is only alerted to the police intervention after the teacher is hospitalized and in the process of making the reported police statement. The school's administration is later asked why they themselves did not call the police. The administration states that the matter was a "complicated situation" given the age of the student.

Even given the violent nature of this situation, the administration was reluctant to call the police due to the potential for unwanted public attention. Schoolteachers need to know that even though acts like this can occur; sometimes school administrations only look out for their own interests. The teacher getting the police involved quickly was the best option and the right thing to do. If a teacher finds him or herself in a situation such as this where a student assaults a staff member, calling the police immediately is the best solution. Student punishments can be dealt with later, but not until the legal authorities are involved and the safety of the teacher and other students is secure.

It's been shown that there are three groups of people who want police intervention more often regarding episodes of physical violence: parents, teachers, and students. Administrators routinely claim that such intervention is not necessary, as they claim to have the skills necessary to intervene and deliver accurate consequences. Sadly, this is not always the case.

In another case study within the same article, a distraught parent boards a school bus and begins to physically assault the bus driver. This is done because the parent is upset that the bus stop is not closer to their home. Very quickly the police are called, and subsequently charge the parent with assault, battery, and trespassing. As this particular case study shows, sometimes there are inconsistencies with how school personnel handle cases of violence, particularly when students or other school employees are assaulted.

The films below are examples of confrontations involving students and teachers. Students can be quick to react when school personnel confiscate personal objects that are illegally held or misused. Often in these situations, teachers can find themselves in compromising situations. My recommendation is to never take anything away from a student. You can ask for the student to hand over the item, but refrain from forcibly taking it from them. Contact a school resource officer and have them remove the item from the student who is refusing to hand it to you.

- https://www.youtube.com/watch?v=V4rxE3YjVJg
- YouTube Search Title: *Student teacher fight: Video shows Santa Monica wrestling coach take down 'weed-selling' student*

- https://www.youtube.com/watch?v=IgfsNGOD0Bg
- YouTube Search Title: *Fight videos at school: Student teacher fight over cell phone at JFK High in Paterson, New Jersey*

As Kajs et al. (2014) states, the mental and emotional toll such acts can take on innocent witnessing parties can negatively impact both school staff and students' frames of mind. Failure to intervene quickly and correctly can prolong these ailments. Failure to report these violent episodes to numerous responsible parties will most certainly make the problem worse. Failure to act in a consistent manner each and every time sends a direct and indirect message that violence is something that can and will be tolerated.

I recommend watching videos such as the ones below and inserting yourself into the situation. While some of these examples are rare and extreme, examine what you would do differently in these situations and think about what you would do to decrease the likelihood of you becoming hurt or falsely accused of wrongdoing.

- https://www.youtube.com/watch?v=QCfYvKe8mrg
- YouTube Search Title: *Student attacks teacher, caught on video. Teacher fights student - compilation*

SUMMARY POINTS FOR CHAPTER 6

- Those who engage in these acts of physical aggression or violence are also likely to be victims of these behaviors themselves.
- School architectural design can either prevent or encourage student related aggression and the potential for physical violence.
- Removal of large-group dynamics or gatherings where students congregate will decrease the likelihood of unwanted physical contact among students.
- Those who engage in dating relationships at young ages tend to be at risk for lower rates of school success and poor mental and emotional maturity.
- Among those who engage in dating relationships within high school (grades nine through twelve), one-forth of students reported thoughts of suicide by the time they were in twelfth grade, while approximately half of students in dating relationships reported physical violence within.
- You'll never be hit if you stand far enough away. Teach students to walk away and get help immediately, regardless of where they are or what the current circumstances may be. Teachers and school staff should do the same.
- If a teacher finds himself or herself in a situation where a student assaults them or another staff member, or where a staff member assaults a student, the solution is to immediately call the police.

7

Sexual Harassment in School

Most national statistics focus on rape when discussing sexual harassment. However, rape by definition is not sexual harassment. Rape stands alone as its own despicable crime. More commonly, numerous forms of sexual harassment tend to occur in K-12 schools. Sadly these cases go largely unreported and unrecognized due to a lack of education and enforcement among both students and school staff. What can complicate a school's response to such forms of sexual victimization is the presence of sexual harassment over social media via cellular devices. Some schools don't believe in enforcing school or state laws with regard to sexual harassment. Unfortunately when it occurs in school or over a cell phone, school administrators and teachers may believe it can be hard to prove, or they may dismiss such behavior as "typical" among school-aged students.

The most common forms of punishable sexual harassment involve the episodes that are typically seen face-to-face with many witnesses. However, if these acts occur casually, in public, or if these behaviors occur in private, they may largely go unreported by the victims or casual observers. Like with most forms of violence, any failure to report sexual harassment perpetuates its very existence. Aggressive sexual behavior that is not stopped immediately will almost always become worse. Remember, schools are made up of adults and children who represent society. Therefore these sexually aggressive behaviors can and do exist within school environments, and many people may not recognize these behaviors for what they truly are—current expressions of lessons learned, and future patterns of disruptive behavior.

PERCEPTIONS OF SEXUAL HARASSMENT

As Charmaraman et al. (2013) reported in their article titled *Is It Bullying or Sexual Harassment: Knowledge, Attitudes, and Professional Development Experiences of Middle School Staff,* school staff members do in fact differ in their beliefs of how bullying and sexual harassment are defined. Many school officials view these two forms of victimization to be different, thus requiring separate punishments. However, having taught middle and high-school health education, I can tell you that these two forms of victimization are equal.

Eom, Restaino, Perkins, Neveln, and Harrington (2015) define sexual harassment as "unwelcome conduct of a sexual nature, which can include unwelcome sexual advances, requests for sexual favors; or other verbal, nonverbal, or physical conduct of a sexual nature" (p.1). Eom et al. (2015) surveyed twelve through eighteen year olds in a Lickert-style survey and asked them about their responses to their exposure to six different forms of sexual harassment:

1. I have been the target of sexual comments, jokes, teasing, gestures or looks/ogling.
2. I have had my clothing pulled in a sexual way.
3. I have had sexual rumors spread about me.
4. I have had my way blocked in a sexual way.
5. I have been touched, grabbed or pinched in a sexual way.
6. I have been shown or given sexual pictures, photographs, illustrations, messages or notes.

Students responded to these categories with answers of *rare, occasional, often* or *very often.* When asked the question "How much do you think sexual harassment happens in your school?" of the 210 students who participated in the survey, fifty-seven (27.5 percent) reported, "It doesn't happen"; seventy-three (35.3 percent) reported, "It happens to only a few people"; thirty-eight (18.4 percent) reported, "It happens to a fair number of people"; thirty-nine (18.8 percent) reported, "It goes on all the time."

Within their study, Eom et al. (2015) reported that 105 students (50.5 percent) had witnessed or seen sexual harassment within their school, sixty-eight students (32.7 percent) said they had not seen it, and thirty-five (16.8 percent) were not sure.

Overall nineteen (9.2 percent) had seen or heard of one instance of sexual harassment, thirty-six (17.5 percent) reported witnessing two to five instances of sexual harassment, forty-four (21.4 percent) said they had witnessed six or more instances in the past year, and 107 (51.9 percent) said they had not witnessed sexual harassment. Additionally 124 (59.6 percent) reported that they had personally experienced sexual harassment. More specifically, forty-four of ninety-two males (47.8 percent) and eighty of 116 females (69.0 percent) had experienced sexual harassment.

In summary, students report that sexual harassment occurs on a semi regular-to-regular basis. Any discrepancy in knowledge about witnessing sexual harassment may be due to a lack of previous knowledge, current education, or students may attribute these behaviors as common school-related peer interactions. This study's data also suggest that students who had experienced sexual harassment were more likely to score higher for psychological impairment than those who had not experienced sexual harassment. Eom et al. (2015) also stated that school-aged girls are the victims of such forms of sexual harassment more often than boys (60 percent girls; 40 percent boys).

SEXUAL HARASSMENT INVOLVING STUDENTS

Some students, teachers, and administrators may allow sexually aggressive behavior to persist not knowing that it's harmful and that it can becomes more aggressive if left unchecked. Specifically within school environments, common sexually harassing behaviors include, but are not limited to the following:

- PDA (public displays of affection)
- Grabbing peers by the waist
- Pulling on the backs of arms until they bruise
- Snapping bra straps
- Grabbing rear ends
- Bumping into one another so as to make contact with body parts
- Forcible hugging
- Making comments about clothing in a sexual manner
- Making comments about what they want to do to another sexually
- Daring one another to make physical contact with another student in a sexual manner

In each instance, school employees should intervene by separating the students and talking to them individually, after class and one at a time, in an effort to educate them on what they were doing and what messages they were sending. If the student in question refuses to comply, or if the severity of the comments or actions requires an alternative approach, I recommend immediately relying on the resource officer and the present discipline policy for punishment. For those situations less severe (a first-time, less aggressive offence), I recommend making sure to state to the student that you can and will resort to the law and the school's discipline policy for any future infraction.

Female students are guilty of sexual harassment as well. Examples tend to involve conversations of a sexual nature regarding sexual acts or body parts, daring friends to engage in sexual acts with other peers; grabbing, ogling, or forcing themselves on another for physical or visual group attention (PDA or fully undressing in locker rooms in front of unsuspecting peers in an effort to make others feel uncomfortable). While these approaches are common among offending females, they are not dissimilar from the approaches of some offending males. For example, PDA is another form of sexual harassment as any students witnessing these behaviors in school are indirectly being harassed. When such acts take place, the sexual act is being forced on the eyes of innocent parties not willing to participate and without their consent, thereby making some bystanders feel uncomfortable. By definition, this too, is sexual harassment.

School staff can also sexually harass students. As underage individuals typically dominate a school's population, such environments can attract predatory adults (male and female) who possess predatory behaviors. Some of these adults become involved in schools for the sole purpose of preying on or controlling those younger than themselves. Many times these cases may not make the local news channels or newspapers because of their direct nature involving underage individuals. However, media outlets can harp on these behaviors and paint a picture of schools as being a harbor for adult predators. Any time these behaviors are seen or even suspected; students, parents, and suspecting school staff members should report these cases to the school's administration and outside legal authorities immediately. Following through until logical legal conclusions are met is a professional response to such serious situations.

Students can also sexually harass school staff. When such offenses occur from a student toward a teacher or other staff members, the offense is usually verbal in nature or written anonymously for a teacher to find. Commenting on how a teacher is dressed, how a teacher's hair looks, how nice a teacher smells, or how body parts look because of the clothing being worn—are all things students can say to a teacher to mask their true intent. Such comments should be discouraged immediately with the offending parties.

By saying, "See me after class," teachers can meet a student in the hallway with witnesses, and they can easily explain how they don't need to be told how they look or how they dress. This becomes the first warning. Then teacher can state to the student that if these comments are made again, the discipline policy will be used for any future infraction. Teachers should end the interaction by asking if the student understands by saying, "Do you understand what I am telling you?" Wait for a "yes" response from the student and then conclude the interaction. Be sure to document in writing what occurred, answering *who, what, where, when, why,* and *how*. Keep this documentation and any future documentation of reported and witnessed behavior for your records.

Again some ineffective school districts may go to great lengths to hide their employee's destructive behaviors from reaching the public. Districts officials may transfer a guilty teacher or school employee from one district to another, or they may even keep that person within the same district, but give him or her a new position. This is typically done in an effort to shield the public from the truth and to silence both the victim and the guilty party.

In any of these examples mentioned above, the first time should be the last time. Contacting the legal authorities, parents, and school administrators immediately should result in the direct firing of guilty school staff and the expulsion of guilty students. Sexual harassment is a serious crime that requires educated explanations, proper prevention, immediate discipline, and legal consequences that exercise the fullest extent of the law.

SEXUAL HARASSMENT AMONG SCHOOL STAFF

If the sexual harassment occurs between staff members, the incident needs to be documented in writing by the offended party. I recommend immediately leaving the room or location where the offense occurred. Then the incident needs to be described to the immediate administrator of the school building, along with each assistant administrator. This way you know that all parties are aware of what has transpired. I recommend emailing all parties while following up with a face-to-face meeting.

An investigation should occur immediately in such situations. If an investigation does not occur and the guilty person remains in his or her position without punishment, then the offended party should fill out a police report. Failure on the part of a schools administration to remove and question the offending individual immediately may result in retribution by the accused and it may further endanger the offended party. This may sound abrupt at first, but schools may be quick to hide such offensive behavior by having both the accuser and offender meet with one another while administrators attempt to settle the incident in a meeting. This too, is an inappropriate response to a serious legal matter. The two parties should never meet again without the authorities present or legal representation (privately hired lawyers and outside detectives, not union officials or union/school district lawyers). This is an example of an incident that occurs in schools that is not a school matter. Upon the occurrence of the infraction, the incident immediately becomes a legal matter that should be handled outside of the school by legal authorities who have no ties to the school district itself.

Correcting offenders on these behaviors can immediately set an appropriate tone for the school's culture. Allowing these acts to occur by not enforcing the rules or the law will most certainly perpetuate the problem. In discussing this topic with other educators within the profession, one example that was shared with me involved a female high-school science teacher and her school's male technology director.

One particular day after school, the school's technology director entered my classroom and asked me how my day went. I told him it was fine, and he wondered if there was anything he could do for me. He seemed as if he wanted something or needed some information I may have had. I said I was fine, but he approached me in a faster manner, now blocking the doorway. Once he was close to me, he told me I had something on my chin and pointed at my face. When I lifted my head up and wiped my chin with my hand, he swiped his finger down my cleavage between my breasts and said, "Whoops." I immediately asked him to leave, and he said he would but only when he was done asking me some personal questions. I immediately left my classroom and went home. The next day I told the administration what had happened, and they said they would handle it. The technology director was not fired. He was simply asked to take another position in another school building within the same district. Sadly he remained in our building for another full workweek until he was assigned to another school. Everyday I was afraid he might return to my classroom.

Clearly this situation was illegal. It was also remarkably dangerous for the teacher, given the time of day and the remote location of an empty classroom. The teacher who was victimized should have told the administration immediately, both verbally and in writing, before leaving the school building. Then, the teacher should have stated that she would not be returning until the technology director was removed permanently. Not letting the school's administration know immediately could have resulted in the victimizer retaliating against the teacher. Had the teacher also gone to the police that same day, the wheels of justice may have moved more quickly, and the odds of this technology director keeping his job within the same school district may have been lower. Sadly, hindsight is always twenty-twenty. Someone who has never experienced such a traumatic episode in a working environment before, nor read about it, may not be able to make these calculated and preventive moves. This is why I recommend the above steps if such an episode ever takes place.

As Lichty, Torres, Valenti, and Buchanan (2008) state, schools are not likely to post their definitions of sexual harassment online or otherwise, thereby not giving everyone a clear sense of expectations or viable punishments. More troubling, as Lichty et al. (2008) stated, even if school sexual harassment policies are available, they rarely incorporate the specified elements that are labeled in federal guidelines. Therefore, schools and the individuals who work within may create their own rules and punishments for such heinous acts. If school personnel fail to intervene immediately and appropriately in sexual-harassment situations, victimizers can chalk up more victims—in particular if these victimizers are in supervisory positions of authority. All school personnel are legally responsible for reporting sexual harassment and sexual crimes to their superiors and the legal authorities regardless of the perpetrator or the victim (school staff or students). Failure to report such episodes can cost a person his or her employment, and licensure as an educator or administrator.

SUMMARY POINTS FOR CHAPTER 7

- School staff members differ on their definitions of what constitutes bullying and sexual-harassment behavior.
- Any discrepancy in knowledge about witnessing sexual harassment may be due to a lack of previous knowledge, current education, or students may consider these behaviors to be common school interactions.

- Even if school sexual-harassment policies are available, they rarely incorporate the specified elements that are labeled in federal guidelines.
- Teachers and school staff members should be taught about the warning signs of sexual abuse, harassment, and unwanted physical contact. Look for bruising behind the arms, handprints, and physical avoidance by students when around their peers as these may be pleas for help.
- Teachers and school staff should always intervene on suspected sexual harassment. Verbal exchanges, touching, pulling or taunting should always be stopped, and the guilty parties should be disciplined and then educated. Guilty parties should then be made to apologize.
- Sexual harassment in any situation should be immediately addressed with authorities, both within and outside of the school. Depending on the nature or frequency, outside local police should be contacted. Every incident should be recorded in writing.
- Refrain from dating or engaging in sexual relationships with coworkers within a shared school environment or district. This also includes dating or engaging in sexual relationships with the parents of students that you or other teachers may have in class. Such associations can be largely viewed as unprofessionalism and these associations may lead to unproductive and dangerous gossip within a school environment.

8

School-Related Drug Use and Associated Factors

As long as drugs have existed they have been present within school environments. In recent years, there have been clear spikes in drug use among students. Drug manufacturers are also taking note of this spike in use. Heroin, synthetic marijuana, and hallucinogenic drugs still remain the less used drugs among school-aged students, as alcohol and marijuana remain the highest. But these harder narcotics and synthetic drugs still find their way into the school environment and well into the student population. The cheaper the drug—the more likely students will try it. The easier the availability—the more curious a student may become.

With the constant presence of drug use in society, any school that proclaims to not be aware of drug use among its students—is in absolute denial of the facts. According to the CDC (YRBS, 2015), over 40 percent of high-school students (grades nine through twelve) have used marijuana at least once, and 23.4 percent are considered chronic users of the drug. In essence, roughly one-quarter of any high school's population can be considered chronic users of marijuana (CDC, 2015). The YRBS also reports that 22.1 percent of high-school students were offered, sold, or given illegal drugs on school grounds.

We know the academic toll drug use can have on students. Students become worse at remembering, comprehending, summarizing, and organizing. Drug use impacts attendance, achievement, and aggression—and drug use influences negative peer associations and isolation. We also know that outdated perceptions of drug use and poor education among students within school are perpetuating its use. These factors may be contributing to an increase in the casual conversations regarding school-aged student drug use.

Schools are notorious for turning a blind eye to drug use. At any time in any school's parking lot, drug-sniffing dogs could search cars and they might catch roughly one-quarter of the student's population. They may even catch teachers and administrators as well. Sometimes, schools work with police infrequently, thereby setting a tone that enforcement of the law is not necessary within such an environment. School officials may even go so far as to tell the school's staff and students the exact day that drug-sniffing dogs or police will be present. This publically shared information may be divulged in an effort to protect the school's public image by discouraging drug possession on a given day.

PERCEPTIONS OF DRUG USE

Norland and DiChiara (1995) examined teachers' perceptions of student drug use and the associated curriculum that is taught to students. Teachers believed that drug education was not necessary and not an impactful approach in the decline of drug use among their students. However, research has stated that associations to school activities and bonding with classmates can account for less drug use among school-aged students. I tend to disagree with both of these statements, and such reports have been largely debunked in recent years.

Health education intends to teach students about the harmful effects of drug use by examining the drugs origins and history, student's pressure to use, and the drugs societal impact, economic impact, political impact, and physical effects. This can provide a more comprehensive approach to drug education that may be absent.

Peer influence to use drugs, as one might assume, plays an enormous role in the ultimate use among students. Washburn and Capaldi (2014) examined male use of marijuana in high school and found many predictors of marijuana use including peer associations, peer discussions related to drug use, deviant behavior, and delinquency. As this existed among freshman in high school, growth in both drug use and negative behavior was observed well into the senior year of high school. In this study, parental monitoring was seen as the largest external factor to discourage use. The school environment, however, was not examined. It's well understood that drug use and the exposure of its presence within a school environment can plague the image of a school and its officials.

The National Institute on Drug Abuse (2010) reports that alcohol is the most widely used drug among high-school students. The older students become, the more likely they are to use. Marijuana use and cigarette use come in a close second, with their use also increasing as students move through high school. The more schools examine these facts, the more readily they can prepare to educate youth about the harmful effects of drug use.

Figure 11: Trends of Various Drug Use for Eighth, Tenth, and Twelfth Graders (The National Institute on Drug Abuse, 2010)

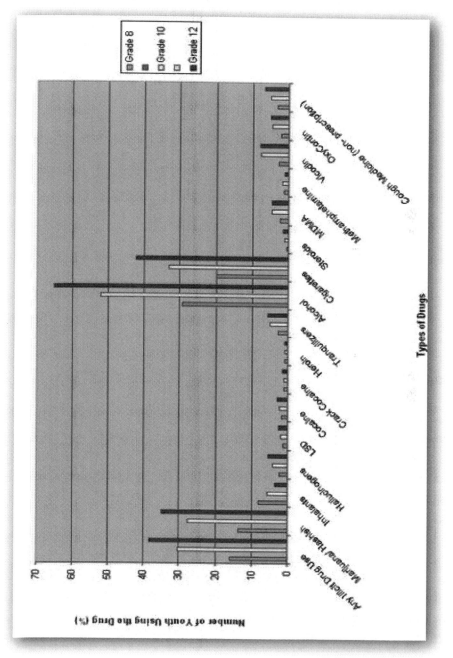

GROUP-ASSOCIATED DRUG USE

Social bonds play a large role in the association of continued drug use, in and around a community (Whaley, Smith, & Hayes-Smith, 2011). Drug use may negatively impact school performance and behavior. Those students who are surrounded by a higher level of peer-driven drug use and social approval are more likely to personally use drugs and demonstrate similar opinions on drug use and the levels of acceptance (Whaley et al., 2011). Students who engage in casual drug use away from the school environment, particularly with marijuana, show high levels of agitation and behavioral issues in school (Finn, 2012). Those students who used marijuana casually were more likely to use in school itself. This use ultimately leads to higher levels of discipline, poor academic performance, dishonesty, and declining school attendance. These characteristics tend to not differ across genders and races (Finn, 2012). Students, who don't use marijuana specifically, tend to show dramatically lower levels of behavioral issues (Finn, 2012).

While direct peer pressure may be overtly believed as the foremost method of drug influence, peer-group modeling as a predictor of future drug use may be underestimated (Mcintosh, Macdonald, & Mckeganey, 2003). Encouragement or personal approval within a peer group may directly influence drug use more so than direct peer pressure (Mcintosh et al., 2003). Drug pressure is likely to be dependent on curiosity and personal decision-making. When students and their peers casually mention drugs, drugs are then likely to be introduced in polite conversations and in friendly tones (Mcintosh et al., 2003), thereby increasing the chances of use and acceptance.

These calm approaches have direct implications for drug educators in reinforcing positive efforts to curb drug use, conversations of such use, and to increase efforts for discussing positive choices (Mcintosh et al., 2003). Students and their peer groups must be educated on the pressures that exist and the commonly used subtle-voice tones that seek to increase drug-use acceptance (Mcintosh et al., 2003). While students who use drugs are *less* likely to seek help and talk to school counselors or school officials, these same drug users are far *more* likely to talk to their peers or friends, thereby potentially perpetuating group use (Jackson et al., 2000).

Denham (2011) reported on the differences between males and females with regard to school-associated sports clubs and their use of alcohol and marijuana. This study discovered that different sports play a larger role in the participation of drug use. The sex and race of the participants are also influential variables. Whether competitive or noncompetitive, students who participated in team sports were more likely to consume marijuana and alcohol and do so as a result of "group clustering" within each sports team or club. Denham (2011) also states that depending on the physical demands of the sport, alcohol and marijuana use may spike or decline. The different cliques within sports teams also played a large role in influencing participation in drug and alcohol use. This study also claims that team-sport participants could positively model healthy habits as well.

If students are in a school-related club and members of the club or sports team are inclined to use drugs, so may go the rest of the group. Peer pressure, including that existing within a school-sanctioned club or group, is undeniably powerful and potentially deadly to the well-being of the participating students. Such school-sanctioned groups and sports teams must be monitored closely and must have a strict zero-tolerance policy for those who are caught with or suspected of using drugs. Or, schools should consider abandoning them altogether.

Duan, Chou, Andreeva, and Pentz (2009) described how peer influence starting in the middle-school years has the biggest impact on a student's use of cigarettes, marijuana, and alcohol. When this influence grows over time, so do peer connections, particularly when students become older. As drug use is commonly a part of these peer connections, preventive education must start early and often for all students. Some programs can tailor more serious efforts to those specific individuals known for their repeated offences or chronic use.

DRUG USE, DATING RELATIONSHIPS, AND ACADEMIC ACHIEVEMENT

It may come as no surprise that as drug use increases among youth or adults, violent and aggressive behaviors also increase. The social groups students associate with may perpetuate this behavior. If members of a group use drugs and behave in aggressive ways verbally, physically, sexually, or otherwise—the rest of the group is likely to follow.

Lormand, Markham, Peskin, Byrd, Addy, Baumler, and Tortolero (2013) examined dating violence among 1,307 middle-school students in an urban school district and found that roughly half of those students reported being physically assaulted by their dating partners. Just as shocking, but not unrealistic, are the associated factors to such violent behavior. Lormand et al., (2013) reported that such violent behavior is associated with numerous negative health effects, particularly drug use. Students who engaged in dating relationships where violence was present were more likely to use drugs individually and collectively within their relationships. A fact to keep in mind is that this study was conducted among middle-school students. As these behaviors persist among middle-school students, there is an increased likelihood of aggression and drug use within dating relationships as these students move into high school.

Many factors play a role in the academic achievement of students in school. Drug use is one of those factors. As drug use increases throughout high school and the pressure to use in social groups increases, the academic potential of students may dramatically drop as a result of this pressure. Whaley et al. (2011) reported that binge drinking is less likely to have an impact on a student graduating from college than a student's use of harder drugs. Ecstasy and methamphetamine use are far more likely to negatively impact a student's chances of graduating from college. Whaley et al. (2011) also stated that the more educated the parents, the less likely their child will use any of these harmful substances. With this education piece in mind, drug education should not be limited to K–12 schools. Colleges and universities have a responsibility to educate their students about these factors as well. Any student receiving this education, regardless of their major course of study, could benefit from such guidance.

Henry (2010) reported on the lowered academic achievement of middle-school students and their relationships to drug use. As student's academic achievement dropped, a significant increase in drug use became evident. Henry (2010) stated that these two occurrences tend to take place at the same time, with one negatively influencing the other. Students in sixth grade who exhibited lowered academic achievement and were drug users, showed no growth in academic achievement as they became older. The flip side of the coin is also true. The more academically successful the student is at a younger age, the less likely he or she is to use drugs and be associated with those who use. However, this does not ensure a complete absence of illicit drug use as the student becomes older.

A final study worth noting involves the connections among drug use, academic achievement, and dating relationships within the adolescent years. Orpinas, Horne, Song, Reeves, and Hsieh (2013) examined dating among middle and high school students, and the connections to drug use and academic achievement. Their study showed that due to the lowered emotional maturity of students, the more frequently students dated; therefore, the less likely they were to be academically successful and the more likely they were to use drugs (marijuana, alcohol, and tobacco). These associations also contributed to higher dropout rates and riskier behavior inside these very relationships. Orpinas et al. (2013) state that students might view dating relationships as a rite of passage in middle school and high school, thereby generating a hidden pressure to engage in such relationships and the habits that can characterize them.

DRUG EDUCATION AND PREVENTION

If you grew up in the 1980s or 1990s, you may be familiar with the DARE program or the Drug Abuse Resistance Education program. The DARE program consisted of a police officer or officers showing up in a local school district, passing out T-shirts that read "Say Nope to Dope," reading through a workbook, and playing games that loosely covered drug-related information. Numerous studies have evaluated the DARE program over the years and they have all found that the program failed to reduce drug use among school-aged children. In essence, the program failed.

The DARE program is one example of many federally funded programs that had positive intentions, but lacked the educational background and follow-up procedures to ensure success. The DARE program has returned in some school districts at the middle school level, and is now called Keepin' It REAL. In the context of the curriculum, REAL is an acronym for *refuse, explain, avoid, and leave*. This is a ten-week program that consists of ten lessons about drugs. Each lesson is roughly forty minutes long and consists of actors on film who are portraying school-aged children who are seemingly struggling with the pressures to use drugs. The lessons culminate with an activity similar to that of the DARE program. I have seen this in action myself. It consists of pizza parties, volleyball games, basketball games, ice cream cones, and T-shirts.

The drug-awareness education and gimmicks haven't changed from the first time they were introduced in the 1980s. The lack of realistic approaches to violence and drug related information is why these programs fail, even today. The gimmicky games I mentioned before are also played at the high school level. If one gimmick or unrealistic approach is used with such a serious subject, it negatively impacts the whole process regarding the intended deterrence. Students can't stand it when a presentation sounds or looks phony in any way.

Singh, Jimerson, Renshaw, Saeki, Hart, Earhart, and Stewart (2011) published an article describing the DARE program that existed in the past and its newly implemented program to date, REAL. The article describes how the old program failed to reach its goals in reducing drug use among students, while the new program has yet to see any positive effects. A major reason behind the failure of the DARE program lies not only in its gimmicky approach to this serious subject matter, but also in the simple fact that the instructors of the program show up periodically for small segments of time. These instructors are not present in the school the way a health education teacher would be. Ultimately, the Real or Dare officers leave once the instruction is over, never to return.

This approach has proved to fail and to be counterproductive to the health and well-being of students within school environments. Such approaches occur not only with the DARE program, but also with any guest speaker who shows up to deliver lengthy content, and is not a full-time teacher inside of the school; particularly if the guest speaker's presentation is the sole exposure students have to the specific present-ed content. Guest speakers can be remarkably impactful, but only if they accompany and conclude the formal instruction delivered by a full-time classroom teacher.

The DARE and REAL programs continue to exist due to financial reasons. They're cheap. This cheap approach allows school to not hire a health education teacher who is certified to teach drug use, risk behaviors, and prevention techniques. However, it's the presence of an effective health education teacher that can remain an influential factor in a student's life. Health teachers can be a daily source for questions, answers, and education. Police officers and uncertified non-full-time instructors will never be as influential, solely due to proximity and time availability. School nurses are in the same category. While they may know associated subjects, they are not formally trained to be classroom teachers.

In his article titled *Sex, Drugs, and the Honor Roll: The Perennial Challenges of Addressing Moral Purity Issues in Schools*, Tupper (2014) describes the reasons why schools struggle to adopt proper and effective prevention methods for drug use and sexual education in America. According to Tupper, this is due to the personal beliefs that both the public, and school officials still have regarding what students need to know. There remains an ancient train of thought that believes that if students are taught about drugs and sex—they will be more likely to engage in both activities. In the twenty-first century, this could not be further from the truth.

Tupper (2014) states that parents and religious leaders still continue to believe that avoidance of factual information is the best prevention method. This has been proven to add to the problem. Such approaches and beliefs by school administrations, parents, and religious leaders, are getting students killed. We as a country are having a hard time getting in front of this ancient way of thinking.

Brener, Wechsler, and McManus (2013) conducted a survey regarding the presence of health education and healthy school environments among forty-eight states in America. The regional areas in America that showed the lowest guidelines for health education and a healthy school environment were in the West and Midwest portions of the United States. Not surprisingly, these are the areas hardest hit by drug addiction and drug abuse in recent years—particularly with regard to heroine, methamphetamine, and opiate narcotic use, sales, and deaths.

Grades six-through-eight health education curriculum regarding drug education is best highlighted within the Bronson, Cleary, and Hubbard's (2011) *Glencoe/McGraw-Hill Health* textbook. In chapter 14 of the 2011 text, lessons and discussions start with the following: drug misuse and abuse; marijuana and other illegal drugs; narcotics, stimulants, and depressants; hallucinogens and inhalants; getting help; and staying drug free. The subjects described within these chapters clearly examine the causes of drug use and provide a bit of history to their origins. This information is also available online and within the high school *Glencoe/McGraw-Hill Health* textbook.

Sometimes this material is not presented to children because of an educator's fear of not knowing enough about the subject, or discomfort about answering student's questions. Many teachers, school officials, parents, religious leaders, and politicians are content with this apparent absence of knowledge. This is not an excuse for not teaching these very important subjects. If states are unwilling to make health education mandatory for all students, separate from physical education instruction, then school districts must address the issue by hiring certified health education teachers who hold a health education bachelor's degree or a degree in a closely related field. Sadly there are students all around America who never receive health-related education on drug awareness, risk factors, abuse, recovery, and effective prevention methods.

I encourage everyone to become involved in communicating with state and local legislators about health education as a mandatory remedy to this absence in drug education. Citizens should demand that certified health education teachers be placed in every school to deliver innovative and realistic education to our youth, from grade five through twelve. I also recommend becoming familiar with your school's health education teacher, if one is present. Talk to them about their curriculum. If the health education teacher fails to take the subject and the curriculum seriously, this may expose another underlying problem.

SUMMARY POINTS FOR CHAPTER 8

- According to the CDC, over 40 percent of high school students' grades nine through twelve have used marijuana at least once.
- There were many predictors of drug use, including peer associations, group discussions, deviant behavior, and delinquency.
- Alcohol is the most widely used drug among high-school students. The older they become, the more likely they are to use. Marijuana use and cigarette use come in a close second, and their use also increases as students move through school.
- Participation in school sports programs can influence ones willingness to use drugs. Whether competitive or noncompetitive, students who participate in sports and sports teams are more likely to consume marijuana and alcohol, and they do so as a result of group clustering within each sports team or club.
- Peer influence starting in the middle school years has the biggest impact on a student's use of cigarettes, marijuana, and alcohol.
- Due to the lowered emotional maturity of students, the more frequently students dated, the less likely they were to be academically successful and the more likely they were to use drugs (marijuana, alcohol, and tobacco). These associations also contributed to higher dropout rates and riskier behavior inside these very relationships.
- The regional areas in America that showed the lowest guidelines for health education and a healthy school environment were in the West and Midwest portions of America.
- Concerned parties and citizens should communicate with state and local legislators about health education as a mandatory remedy to this absence in drug education. Demand that certified health education teachers be placed in every school to deliver innovative and realistic education to our youth.

9

Rethinking School-Sanctioned Traditions and Activities

In environments where cooperative learning should flourish, competition is sometimes used as a measuring stick for academic success. Schools compete with one another regarding sports programs, academia, and state-standardized test scores. As school districts and school officials can readily perpetuate competition, these learned behaviors easily find their way into classrooms where students are forced to participate. Such practices can potentially lead to peer division, segregation, cheating, and hostility.

For over a century, school and competition have been closely associated with one another. The manifestation of sports programs within schools has led school administrators and teachers to believe that competition is a viable instructional method that can harvest positive results. However, the opposite may be true. Competitive strategies within numerous locations inside of a school environment may in fact be antecedents to violent behavior that lead to lowered academic success. As Albert Einstein stated, "Education is what remains after one has forgotten what one has learned in school."

COMPETITION AND ACADEMIC ACHIEVEMENT

While competition and academic success can be positively linked to one another, most scholars admit that competition should be used sparingly, if at all. Wilkins (2012) states that boys are more likely to engage in competition and tend to do so more readily among their own friends, while girls are more likely to resist competition in classroom settings. With schools placing such an emphasis on competition as a classroom instructional strategy, the clear presence of winners and losers may negatively individualize or isolate success (Wilkins, 2012). Competition can also have negative effects on learning, and it can increase levels of student frustration (Chang, Chuang, & Ho, 2013). Even though some students or cultures may be drawn to competition, the presence of competition or forcing competition on a student population may in fact be culturally insensitive (Chang et al., 2013).

When students from different cultures don't have competition within their family or cultural history, they are not likely to participate (Jameson, 2007). Students also recognize the levels of enthusiasm among their peers when witnessing competition, and many can find such behaviors to be immature (Jameson, 2007). For example, French students tend to be more theatrical and enjoy collaboration and cooperation where different parties have different roles, all while working toward a common goal. American students tend to view classrooms as competitive environments, much like a stadium, in which the goal is to outperform their peers in a public display (Jameson, 2007). In either case, it's clear that one culture can support cooperation or competition more than another.

Competition within the classroom can also present obstacles to effective classroom management. With winners and losers being quickly defined in competitive settings; verbal taunts, name-calling, and physical intimidation can accompany such activities. Instead of students learning information and working cooperatively, peer aggression and hostility may become commonplace, thereby leading to a lack of interest in the activity or the subject matter altogether. Anderman and Murdock (2007) state that cheating brings about numerous negative behaviors as well, some of which are perpetuated by the very activities involving competition. Anderman and Murdock (2007) state that competition is perhaps the single most toxic ingredient in a classroom, and it's also a reliable predictor of cheating.

Numerous authors and scholars believe that performance, problem solving, and personal relationships are damaged as a result of competition in the classroom, as compared to using cooperation. Other studies suggest that competition directly undermines intrinsic motivation, thereby intellectually humiliating the participants forced to engage in such activities. Orosz, Farkas, and Roland-Lévy (2013) state that many other studies have said the opposite, and that competition can be productive and foster positive relationships. However, Orosz et al. (2013) also stated that competition could bring about hypersensitivity to accomplishments. Such sensitivity surrounding classroom competition can lead to higher occurrences and thoughts of cheating (Orosz et al., 2013).

While some teachers and school officials view competition as an enjoyable activity and one that is absent of negative thoughts or actions, other students may become more driven by the need to win at all costs. These behaviors are evident within companies, sports programs, and competitive businesses where profit, public success, and money are motivators. Ineffective school administrators, school district officials, and teachers are not free from these negative influences where the competitive nature to succeed can bring out the worst in those claiming to be effective leaders.

Perhaps the best solution is to minimize or completely remove competition in the classroom or school environment as a possible predictor of violent behavior. While some competition could be used sparingly, observing and recording students' and teachers' perceptions of competition in the classroom and throughout the school environment—may help inform teachers and administrators of a problematic instructional practice. If one is interested in avoiding the risks associated with the implementation and related consequences of competition in the classroom, its permanent removal and absence within school environments may be the safest solution.

SCHOOL-SANCTIONED ATHLETICS

School-sanctioned athletics have also been a part of school environments for well over a century. The violent toll these activities can take on students is sparsely reported on, yet these very activities are rarely removed. While many of these programs receive public support from community members and financial donors, resources totaling in the tens of millions of dollars are spent on supporting these programs and related facilities. This occurs while some classrooms themselves fail to possess up-to-date technological tools for today's learning and instruction. The distractions these activities create may also send a violent and aggressive message regarding their perceived over-importance. These messages can easily insult the majority of the student population who are nonparticipants.

As academic achievement remains a school's bottom line, some view the presence of sports in school as a necessity, a predictor to higher academic achievement, and an element that lowers violent crime. Veliz and Shakib (2012) stated in their study regarding interscholastic sports participation that while student participation in school-related interscholastic sports programs decreased serious violent crime on school grounds, it was *not* a predictor of decreasing minor violent crime within a school environment. The authors also admit that gang-related activity was not measured in their study, as competitive sports programs can sometimes foster a gang-like mentality among their members. The authors also failed to discuss how some students who participate in sports programs or after-school activities may receive a free pass, or more leniencies regarding schoolwork from parents, school staff members, and coaches.

Taliaferro, Rienzo, and Donovan (2010) reported that participation within school-sanctioned sports programs contributed to violent behavior among some participating students, but also that race is indicative of the type and frequency of violent behavior. Taliaferro et al. (2010) reported that while students who play sports can engage in healthy behaviors that increase the likelihood of personal well-being, many students show a decrease in healthy behaviors, particularly among participating minority students. Taliaferro et al. (2010) suggested that coaches and school officials should come to agreements regarding the onset of violent behaviors, and that they should work to diminish the specific activities that lead to negative actions.

Kreager (2007) examined the relationships between contact sports and violent behavior. Kreager's (2007) analysis suggested that football players and wrestlers, as opposed to baseball, basketball, tennis, and other athletes—are significantly more likely than nonathletic males to be involved in a serious fight. Kreager (2007) also stated that those students who are friends with football players and don't play football themselves are also more likely to fight, as opposed to those students who don't associate with sports whatsoever.

Coaches and other school employees also share responsibility when it comes to violent behavior within sports programs. This violence shows itself in many ways. For example, now that high school sports are so readily aired on national television programs around the world, many coaches may feel the pressure to become one of these popularized teams who receive national attention. This pressure brings with it an intensity level that many students can't handle, and most students may want nothing to do with.

Shields (1999) reported that the vast majority of high-school athletic directors stated that physical intimidation, verbal intimidation, and physical violence were serious problems within sports programs. Shields (1999) reported that football, basketball, and soccer were the three sports where the above violent characteristics were the most problematic. Shields (1999) also reported that the coaches of these sports perpetuated these negative characteristics, and such behaviors are potentially seen as antecedents to future aggressive behavior, away from the fields of play. Perhaps more telling regarding the acceptance levels of such behavior, is that roughly half (53.3 percent) of the students who play these sports view these violent behaviors as acceptable and believe them to be actions that accompany standard participation (Shields, 1999).

The contextual settings, attitudes, pressures, and coaching behaviors are all factors that influence aggression and violence related to sports programs. As Shields (1999) stated,

Pep rallies, team cheers and school atmosphere, coupled with a coach who berates officials throughout the game, may create a context in which intimidation and violence by athletes are viewed as appropriate. Aggression can also be learned and various social-psychological factors help maintain this type of behavior while the behavior becomes legitimized over time. Tremendous pressure on the athletes to win can and often does come from several sources, and the message may be to win at all costs. Although it must be acknowledged that officials, parents, peers and others clearly exert influence, ultimately coaches are the ones who allow, encourage or teach their players to use verbal and physical intimidation tactics (p. 22).

Students who play sports may also attend signing days where they commit to attend a college or university under a sports scholarship. These students are sometimes placed in front of the whole school in an effort to show off whom the school believes to be the best of the best. Such an illusionary importance on these activities quickly ostracizes the majority of the student population. Signing days are typically conducted during the school day, during instructional time, and some of them are televised. Perhaps such activities should be done behind closed doors and during the weekend, so that instructional time is not wasted or interrupted, and the presence of nonparticipating students is not required.

When schools place this kind of importance on such activities and the students who play them, the frustration and aggression levels of the majority of a student population can increase. When student athletes engage in violent behaviors either on or away from the fields of play, they can often be given a free pass by the school, their coaches, and society. It's these very influential adults themselves who may be teaching and supporting these detrimental behaviors.

Perhaps the violence prevention suggestion here would be for pre-service teachers to think about distancing themselves from sports programs and coaching all together. It's necessary to hold all students accountable for their detrimental behavior, regardless of the school-related sports team they affiliate themselves with. If teachers align themselves with such groups within school environments, and laws are broken or favoritism occurs, they may find themselves regretting such associations. Guilt by association can get a teacher in hot water and destroy their career. So the simple question has to be asked—is a teacher's career about coaching or education?

Perhaps in the future, K–12 schools will distance themselves from athletics and view their presence in school as an unnecessary part of academia. Perhaps it's time for the funds, donations, participation, and organization of school-sanctioned sports to be handed over to a mayor's office or a chamber of commerce within towns and cities across America. K–12 schools might then refocus themselves as academic institutions that are free from sports-related activities. Schools might even be less violent as a result. As it turns out, many schools across America have already accomplished this with great success.

PHYSICAL EDUCATION
Physical education dates back to the mid-nineteenth century in Europe. This course was constructed to increase physical health among school-aged students in an effort to prepare them for war, if necessary. By the mid-twentieth century, America had adopted over four hundred physical education majors of study and incorporated such lessons within schools across the country. Now, physical education's presence is sometimes used as another political tool in an effort to decrease what some officials describe as an obesity epidemic among teenagers.

The vast majority of schools that have physical education will insist on student participation. Some students can opt out of these courses given a particular physical, mental, or other limitation that makes attending problematic or not feasible. However, most students are forced to attend, have their ever-changing body sizes measured and compared (body mass index/BMI), participate in games, and "dress out" in front of their peers as major requirements for passing these courses. As described earlier, competition, division, unnecessary comparisons, and physical limitations can all be predictors of violent behavior.

Body mass index, or BMI, is another measurement tool commonly used within physical education classes for self-comparison over time, and peer-comparison immediately. The equation to calculate this measurement includes an individual's mass or weight in pounds, multiplied by 703, and then divided by his or her height in feet and inches. BMI does not take into account age, even though some measurement calculators claim this to be the case. This formula is even used at the elementary school level among kindergarten students. In many cases, these measurements are taken while other students are physically present, thereby making this falsely believed statistic a topic of gossip among a student population. Letters can be sent home to parents telling them that their child is underweight, overweight, or obese, and that their child may soon suffer from major health problems as a result.

This poorly used false measurement has directly contributed to the mental and emotional decline of students within school settings. Many parents have pulled their children out of their local school districts due to the presence of this measurement alone. A student's self-esteem and self-concept can be seriously altered while attending physical education classes and undergoing the measurements that are commonly associated with such attendance. Students can be pinned against one another in a never-ending battle of comparison that rarely ends peacefully. Body image, eating disorders, and other forms of mental and emotional abuse, can all stem from physical education attendance—even among those who may be seen or viewed as physically active, strong, or popular.

Beyond these examples, what can make the presence of physical education in schools especially troubling, is that within this very environment, every type of leading contributor to violent behavior is likely to be present in one concentrated area on a daily basis, year after year, even if properly supervised. In its simplest form, physical education instructors are outnumbered, as their classes typically hold the largest number of students at any one time. Therefore it's impossible to monitor every student's behavior or action.

Atkinson and Kehler (2012) stated that students in Canada are reporting a dramatically increased lack of interest in physical education attendance within schools and that there are major sociological reasons for such thoughts. Atkinson and Kehler (2012) reported that students readily described how physical education classes are dominated by higher levels of participation among those seen as popular, or physically strong and athletic. This perpetuates limited participation as the popular students are routinely selected to be team captains or lead contributors on a team, thereby potentially ostracizing those who are seen as incapable. As stated earlier, students report that coaches themselves are the lead contributors to such masculinizing behavioral reinforcement. Coaches can go so far as to ridicule students who are incapable of higher levels of physical exertion, and they tend to do so without reservation (Atkinson & Kehler, 2012). Perhaps more enlightening, is that students also reported wanting more health education in a classroom setting, as opposed to attending physical education classes (Atkinson & Kehler, 2012).

The issues associated with physical education rarely address self-identity, bullying, and trauma that are common within such environments (Atkinson & Kehler, 2012). While many physical education environments are dependent on physical prowess and masculinity driven norms, Anderson (2012) claims that physical education classes are becoming more inclusive and are doing so with those students who associate as homosexual. While this particular study only occurred within one school, and asked only seventeen teenagers, these teenagers claimed that more inclusion was occurring with differing students, and many different students were participating in physical education regardless of their sexuality, masculinity level, or physical ability (Anderson, 2012).

While some students may see physical education as beneficial, these responding students may not see the abuse that is actually occurring. Participating students may ultimately see aggressive behavior as acceptable within such environments. While this study painted a pleasant picture of physical education classes, some students within these environments and within this very study may view physical education as their favorite class for negative reasons. This may be due to their willingness to put down their peers or see their own physical activity level as their strongest personal attribute.

Bejerot, Edgar, and Humble (2011) reported that students are likely to be victimized if seen as clumsy or lacking physical attributes as compared to their more athletic peers. Bejerot et al. (2011) also reported that these victimized students are likely to be bullied long after physical education classes end, leading to a continuation of bullying behaviors in other classes and other school locations. This also occurs due to their reduced motor skills, particularly if these students are labeled as autistic, or possessing attention deficit hyperactivity disorder (ADHD). This study shows yet another aspect of violent behavior that exists within physical education classes that may divide students, thereby increasing the likelihood of conflict and violent behavior.

Perhaps the most detrimental factor existing within physical education classes— involves the long-standing tradition of students changing clothes or dressing out in front of one another within a locker-room setting. Dressing out is commonly a requirement for passing physical education classes. If students refuse to change their clothes in front of one another, they are typically subjected to a lowered grade, or even a failing grade from the instructor. The direct message being sent is that regardless of their physical maturity, level of comfort, previous or current sexual background, gender identification, or disability; all students are required to take their clothes off in front of their peers.

What remains hypocritical of school systems is that if this requirement were posed upon a school's adult staff, the adults would most certainly refuse and file a lawsuit. Yet schools require children of all ages, races, gender identities, and physical formations to engage in this act, unless parents opt their children out of physical education classes. Very commonly school officials may say that all students have a safe place to change their cloths with privacy if they wish for it. But, most people who have stepped inside of K–12 locker rooms know otherwise. There are minimal stalls that offer even less privacy, and when those students choose to change out of the sight of their peers they are commonly victimized for doing so without repercussion.

Grades six through eight are typically the first grades forced to engage in this practice. Some female and male students remove every article of their own clothing without privacy. Some do so willingly in an effort to exert their physical maturity upon their peers without hesitation. Such behaviors could be compared to exhibitionism, which as discussed earlier, is a psychological disorder that can be an antecedent to violent and aggressive behavior that potentially leads to sexual promiscuity at an early age. Varying forms of sexual assault, sexual battery, sexual harassment, rape, sodomy, and other heinous acts—can and do occur inside locker rooms within K–12 schools.

Schools across America also have gay and lesbian physical-education teachers who are tasked with monitoring students of the same sex within locker room settings as students undress. If the tables were turned, the school would never allow a straight male or straight female to watch the opposite sex undress within a locker room setting. This is yet another reason why simply removing dressing out as a requirement can alleviate any discrepancy in teacher hiring, firing, or placement of physical education teachers. In this case, locker rooms don't need to exist anymore. This would allow any qualified individual regardless of age, gender or sexual preference to teach physical education without being subjected to discrimination or unfair treatment. The removal of locker rooms may alleviate any misconceptions, while allowing qualified responsible adults to remain in their physical education positions.

Some school districts may also require students to participate in very specific forms of physical activity. For example, in discussing these violent incidents with other educators around the country at education conferences, some have reported to me that swimming is a mandatory physical activity within their school district. One example I was introduced to by a concerned educator in Connecticut, involved a requirement that made every male student wear the same skintight speedo swimsuit and every female wear the same skintight one-piece swimsuit. This was a district requirement regardless of the student's gender identification, physical size, weight, or physical maturity. Failure to participate would result in an incomplete or failing grade for the course, thereby leading to the absence of a graduation requirement. With such practices existing within some school environments and school districts, it may be hard to explain to students, parents, and the general public how schools can always ensure safety and academic fairness. As a result, more and more students in K–12 schools are fulfilling their physical education requirements online. This is not an accident.

PROM AND HOMECOMING ACTIVITIES

The histories of prom and homecoming activities are very similar. The first dances of this nature were held at the collegiate level during the 1800s. These traditions are meant to signify the end of one significant time period in one's life and the beginning of a new chapter. These events typically take place at the beginning and end of an academic year, and they are traditionally held for those who are about to graduate from their academic institution. These traditions also exist around the world on almost every continent.

Popular culture has mocked and ridiculed the activities related to prom and homecoming for decades. Over twenty-eight major motion pictures have been made in America depicting the relationship that schools, teenagers, and adults have to prom and homecoming activities. Many more movies and TV shows have brief depictions of prom dances specifically—and the pressures and behaviors commonly associated with these traditions. Some major motion pictures have even been made more than once. Two examples are *Prom Night,* which was made in both 1980 and 2008; and the movie *Carrie,* which was made in 1976, 2002, and 2013, both of which are categorized as horror films. In a 2016 TV episode of *Family Guy,* titled "Run, Chris, Run" on the Fox network, the oldest son Chris Griffin is voted prom king for the real reasons some are voted for such an arbitrary title. The whole episode mocks the school system as it describes the detrimental behaviors of both the students and the school staff regarding their willful and harmful participation in this tradition. It's a perfect example of *sad, but true.*

The factors associated with prom, homecoming, and traditional school-sanctioned dances can be remarkably detrimental to the students, their families, and the surrounding communities. These dances and traditions have been the subject of numerous discriminations toward students. LGBTQ students have been prohibited from attending these dances or bringing dates. School administrators have inconsistently deemed school dance attire inappropriate across participating countries. Disabled students have been thrown out for bringing their older siblings or family members as dates. Students have been barred from brining their siblings or dates that are members of the military. Students make social-media posts pressuring their potential dates to attend, while they film the attempt in an effort to elicit a positive response, thereby displaying the characteristics of narcissism and exhibitionism. These examples make the evening news every spring and fall, every year like clockwork. However, deadly outcomes associated with prom and homecoming nights can sometimes be hidden from the national media in an effort to prolong these very traditions that many feel to be outdated, inappropriate, and unsafe.

In an article written by Charleton Kendrick titled, *Prom, death and sexual assault: Helping your teen make safe, smart decision: The talk, the ride, the connection, the offer,* he describes the very points as to why high schools around America may want to permanently eliminate prom and homecoming activities forever. Table 5 describes facts referenced within the article that are worth knowing. Table 5 could also be used to encourage school districts to abolish the presence of such activities. The statistics are both predictable, and detrimental to the well-being of the students, their families, the sanctioning schools, and willing participants.

Table 5: Prom, Death, and Sexual Assault: Helping Your Teen Make Safe, Smart Decisions, the Talk, the Ride, the Connection, the Offer (Kendrick, 2013)

1.   Teen traffic deaths during prom-season weekends are higher than at any other time of the year.
2.   According to the National Highway Traffic Safety Administration, for the past several years during prom weekends, approximately three hundred teens have died in alcohol-related car accidents.
3.   Also according to the NHTSA, one in three children under age twenty-one who died in alcohol-related accidents died during prom and graduation season.
4.   An American Medical Association study reported that 10 percent of parents believed it is appropriate and safe for underage teens to attend both prom and graduation parties where alcohol is served, if a parent is present.
5.   Most date rapes and sexual assaults against girls are alcohol and drug related.
6.   A US Department of Health and Human Services national survey reported that 39 percent of high-school senior boys considered it acceptable to force sex on a girl who is intoxicated by alcohol or high on drugs.

Such associations can cause division within schools, and yet these facts rarely discourage school districts from ending these traditions for good. The pettiness associated with these rituals can lead students to feel isolated and embarrassed. The actions students may take to cope with such school-sanctioned pressures may also be detrimental to their personal health. Teen suicide, sexual promiscuity, teen pregnancy, teen drug use, teen alcohol abuse, binge drinking, sexual assault, copious amounts of peer pressure, and other negative health-related factors tend to increase around these very activities that the schools themselves emphasize as being rites of passage. Schools even reenact prom night tragedies during classroom instructional time in an effort to deter students from engaging in the same activities that can lead to deadly consequences. Such displays during normal classroom instructional time could be seen as a blatant admission that the school itself sanctions the very activity that can lead to risky behaviors and student deaths.

So why do schools and school districts still view prom activities as a "positive school experience?" When students within a school die or are hurt as a result of these school-sanctioned events, do the schools ever take the blame for setting them up? Some schools even go to great lengths to make prom and homecoming dances inclusive for all, including those within a school who may not normally be invited. However, keep in mind that the vast majority of every school's population never attends prom or homecoming dances.

Sometimes it's the lack of real inclusion that can send the wrong message. For example, Clark (2016) wrote in a southwest Ohio newspaper, the *Journal News*, an article titled, *Daylight Prom a magical event in Butler, Warren counties*. Within this article, Clark (2016) described how some local school districts were hosting a "Daylight Prom" for their special-needs students while the special-education teachers within these buildings facilitated these activities.

For this daylight prom inside special-education classes, during a normal school day within a high school, students who had special needs were asked to wear nice cloths (dresses, slacks, tuxes, corsages, boutonnieres, etc.) to school during a normal school day. The teachers transformed their special-needs classroom into a prom dance hall and allowed their special-needs students to dance with one another. Clark (2016) stated, "Their prom dates were their parents, siblings, and special-needs classmates."

While this may sound innocent to some, as the importance of an event like this is in the eye of the beholder, such an activity may create the very thing that most teachers and school administrators are trying to avoid—students making fun of other students while not being inclusive. This "Daylight Prom" activity may also look odd to the casual observing student. As the vast majority of the school's population would enter the school building, the special-needs students would be dressed for prom. Immediately the other students might wonder what special event was going on in their school that day. The word might then travel around school that "the special-needs students are having their own prom dance in their classroom." When such things are known and said among the vast majority of the school's population, does anyone believe that positive, nonviolent things are going to be said or gossiped about?

It's an activity such as this where these participating teachers may be setting up their special-needs students to be made fun of, either to their faces or behind their backs. Is the school saying that special-needs students aren't allowed to go to prom because of their disabilities? Are they saying that special-needs students need dates to attend a prom or that they would never be asked to attend in the first place? Are adults teaching these special-needs students that they don't qualify for regular activities that exist within the school? Are teachers and school officials segregating these special-needs students more so than they already do? Is this really the definition of inclusion in an era where schools claim they are attempting to become more inclusive? Is this really the definition of inclusion?

The school staff members who organized the activity were quoted in the *Journal News* as saying,

> It's very important for individuals with disabilities to experience every facet of high school life, and many teens with disabilities are not invited to proms and events. Prom is a rite of passage and very important for all people to have this life experience. This is amazing and the realistic nature of this prom means we are providing something for the students that many of their parents never thought they would be a part of. We're providing them with a lifetime milestone with this event (p. B-2).

Prom is not a lifetime milestone. Prom is not a rite of passage. These activities can hurt people, destroy relationships, and force teenagers on one another physically, and in unhealthy ways that are uninvited and regrettable. In the case of the Daylight Prom—and any prom or homecoming dance—the school is segregating students, setting them up to be made fun of, and creating an illusion of importance around a prolonged, unhealthy, outdated ritual. In my professional opinion, schools should remove the very activities that increase school violence and division, and any events that are shown to increase crime-related activities. This way, special-needs students and all students won't be misled by their teachers, their peers, or their communities into thinking that prom is an important "lifetime milestone."

Another activity that is perpetuated by schools and always talked about during prom and homecoming season, is the voting of the traditional prom and homecoming king and queen. This is another activity that pits students against one another in a superficial voting process that typically awards the crowns to those students deemed the most popular or the most attractive. Sometimes, students may vote for a special-needs student to be prom and homecoming king or queen. Then the special-needs student wins the contest. While most schools report such an occurrence as an "act of kindness" that presents itself in the local newspaper or televised evening news story, behind the scenes there are disappointed students who placed enormous pressure on themselves to win. Some students may even vote for their special-needs peers to win the contest so that the "popular" or "attractive" students don't win. So who really wins? Does any of this sound healthy?

When a local or national news channel reports on a special-needs student winning the prom or homecoming king or queen contest, understand that this may have been done intentionally to anger other students, all while attempting to embarrass or manipulate the special-needs student. Even though the special-needs student tends to believe that this recognition is authentic (and sometimes it is), it may not be. In situations such as this, school officials, parents, and students may know the real motivations. Again, while some news channels report on these occurrences as acts of kindness, the truth may actually be far worse.

Such an activity could be equated to the "superlative awards" that schools so commonly embrace as another rite of passage and a memorable moment (i.e., students vote for best smile, best hair, most likely to succeed, most likely to be president, best athlete, most likely to be a supermodel, etc.). At the risk of oversimplification, these school-sanctioned activities hurt people's feelings, while schools place an illusionary importance on superficiality. They have absolutely noting to do with education.

Again in the interest of academic evolution and creating a non-divisive, inclusionary school climate and environment, the immediate elimination of such activities and outdated rituals is essential to the well-being and evolution of all schools, educators, students, and their families. If dances and related activities are going to exist, creating empathy, inclusion, and situations where everyone is invited may be more beneficial to every student within the school environment. Segregating students within school-related activities perpetuates division that is all too common within schools already. Fair and just implementation or overall elimination of these practices, would truly be the definition of inclusion that schools claim to be aiming for.

Scholarly academic research has yet to examine the specific areas of prom, homecoming, and these school-sanctioned traditions. Cross-comparisons could be developed regarding schools that maintain these traditions, those schools that have removed them, and those that have never had them to begin with. The detrimental effects school-sanctioned activities are having on the well-being of students and their academic achievement could also be measured. These potential antecedents to lowered academic performance and aggressive behavior should be researched and reported on in the future.

SUMMARY POINTS FOR CHAPTER 9

- Competitive strategies within school environments may in fact be antecedents to violent behavior that leads to lowered academic success.
- The clear presence of winners and losers may negatively individualize and isolate student success.
- Cheating brings about numerous negative behaviors, some of which are perpetuated by the very activities involving competition.
- While some competition could be used sparingly, observing and recording students' perceptions of competition in the classroom and within the school environment may help inform teachers and administrators of a problematic instructional practice.
- Student participation in school-related interscholastic sports programs is not a predictor in decreasing minor violent crime within school.
- Athletic directors of high-school sports report that physical intimidation, verbal intimidation, and physical violence are serious problems within sports programs.
- The contextual settings, attitudes, pressures, and behaviors of coaches are factors that influence aggression and violence related to sports programs.
- Body image, eating disorders, and other forms of mental and emotional abuse can all stem from physical-education attendance, even among those who may be seen or viewed as physically active, strong or popular.
- Victimized students are likely to be bullied long after physical-education classes end, leading to a continuation of bullying behaviors in other classes and other school locations.
- Varying forms of sexual assault, sexual battery, sexual harassment, rape, sodomy, and other heinous acts can and do occur inside locker rooms within K–12 schools.

- Teen suicide, sexual promiscuity, teen pregnancy, teen drug use, teen alcohol abuse, binge drinking, sexual assault, copious amounts of peer pressure, and other negative health-related factors tend to increase around activities that the schools themselves emphasize as being a rite of passage (prom, home-coming, sports, club participation).
- Schools should create a non-divisive, inclusionary school climate and environment. The immediate elimination of such petty activities and outdated rituals may be essential for student and school-related violence prevention
- Schools that focus more on music and the arts as an alternative to the above activities, with an absence of competition, may provide their students a more positive experience.

10

Workplace Bullying Within Educational Environments

Workplace bullying is a phenomenon that is ever present within numerous working environments. Much like the word *bullying,* workplace bullying may have originated within schools themselves. However, vast research focuses on the professions of nurses, doctors, and business professionals regarding one's exposure to workplace bullying. Like most working environments where the numbers of employees are elevated and the need for quality output is a necessity, people may be more likely to witness workplace bullying or become the direct victims themselves. Schools are not free from the presence of workplace bullying. In fact, workplace bullying may be perfectly exemplified within school-based environments.

Namie and Namie (2009) state in their very important book, *The Bully at Work,* that 72 percent of all workplace bullying comes from bosses, while 18 percent comes from peers, and 10 percent comes from the bottom up. Most employees within a work environment may enjoy relative autonomy or small-group collaboration that fuels their motivation in positive ways. But when someone feels that he or she has been slighted, overlooked, or even demoted, that person may engage in vengeful behavior in an effort to exude his or her will or knowledge of a task. This creates opportunities for intimidation.

Vega and Comer (2005) defined workplace bullying as a pattern of destructive and generally deliberate demeaning of coworkers or subordinates that reminds us of the activities of the schoolyard bully. Within this very definition, one may find the true origin of the phrase and the acts that define such hostile behavior. While workplace bullying has been defined many ways and definitions can be easily referenced, I would define workplace bullying as; *any interpersonal behavior within a working or learning environment that seeks to intimidate, demean, ridicule, or force compliance in an effort to harm, manipulate, or distort the truth—for personal gain, control, or status.* In all working definitions of the phrase, the core of workplace bullying is the need or attempt to harm in the interest of gaining control, typically due to feelings of inadequacy.

Pre-service teachers within teacher-education programs need to be taught about the characteristics of workplace bullying. Teacher-education professors should address this very important topic in depth. Prevention methods and reporting strategies could easily be taught in a variety of classes in an effort to realistically prepare future educators. This education could show pre-service teachers what they are likely to see within educational working environments and how the law may or may not help them avoid unjust treatment at the hands of those who engage in such destructive behaviors. As musician Chris Cornell once wrote, "Hands are for shaking, not for tying."

PERCEPTIONS OF WORKPLACE BULLYING

Joiner, Hall, and Richardson (2015) reported that college students' exposure to the knowledge of workplace bullying is remarkably low, and that given their immediate interest in entering the workforce upon graduation, such an education may prepare them for what may be inevitable. Joiner et al. (2015) stated that roughly half of all men and women experience workplace bullying while employed. The same is true for those who victimize. Roughly half of all men and women bully others within their places of work (Joiner et al., 2015). A major misconception is that men only bully women and women only bully women. This statement could not be further from the truth. Bullies and their targets are made up of all ages, races, ethnicities, physical attributes, and gender identities. Workplace bullies embody a pattern of behaviors, not a particular physical look.

Specifically regarding college students' perceptions of workplace bullying, Dr. Namie and his Workplace Bullying Institute gave permission to Joiner et al. (2015) to use their survey. Within this survey, students were asked about their age, the perpetrator's rank in the workplace, perceived perpetration, individuals supporting the perpetrator, forms of mistreatment, health-related conditions as a result of mistreatment, and actions taken to address the mistreatment. Joiner et al. (2015) reported that within 67 percent of the cases where mistreatment was reported, the employer did nothing. Twenty one percent indicated that the perpetrator remained in his or her position while adverse employment pressure was placed on the victim (i.e., continued intimidation, pressure to leave, threatening job loss). Joiner et al. (2015) stated that workplace bullying has massive implications for workplace morale, personal and group health, quality of life, and the well-being of an organization's culture.

The presence of workplace bullying within school-based environments is both cyclical and inbred. This is to say that the consequences of workplace bullying and its presence stem from the top down and throughout a school district. If those in charge (superintendents, assistant superintendents, HR directors, investigators, school-level administrators) conduct such negative practices and get away with it, this is largely due to these same behaviors being perpetuated and supported among the masses.

Given that workplace bullying is not necessarily against the law and little to no laws exist on the books to enforce such mistreatment, college students and pre-service teachers should educate themselves about the rights they have within school environments and other workplaces. I personally recommend taking educational steps upon your immediate employment within a school district. For example, I recommend hiring, for a small fee, an education lawyer in your area or outside of your area for a legal consultation. This process involves a face-to-face meeting where you introduce yourself and tell the lawyer about your background and your current place of employment. Ask the lawyer about any past legal troubles your hiring school district has had, if any. The lawyer may not be able to tell you, in which case a simple Google search ahead of time may expose a pattern of behavior worth knowing.

Ask the lawyer about what you are legally obligated to do in specific cases involving physical contact between students and staff members, sexually related behaviors, unethically changed grades, and other abuses—and which parties you should report these infractions to. Most lawyers will tell you to not trust the administrators. They may tell you to report the incident in person and in writing to the school's administration, and then to report the incident to the police. This can be great advice.

Such legal advice is rarely sought until it's too late. Taking this preemptive step can give you a sense of control with accurate information that may protect you in the future. At the very least, it may give you solace in knowing that you covered every base accurately. In this case, as in most cases, knowledge is power—particularly when it comes to documenting, witnessing, or being personally subjected to workplace bullying.

Another sad fact regarding the presence and perceptions of workplace bullying is the lack of enforcement from those that should be responsible for creating organizational well-being. As Cowan (2011) states, many HR (human resource) departments have similar policies that enforce such negative behaviors, and they can hold guilty parties accountable. However, these policies may contradict one another, and HR's personal perceptions may vary on the presence of their own policies. The policy language used may not specifically state the word *bullying*, as some organizations use phrases such as *codes of conduct* or *harassment*. Regardless of the situation or terminology used by school district officials or other organizations, by asking an education lawyer outside of your school district such questions, future teachers can gain an understanding of what rights they have and how they can be protected in the workplace.

Sadly, as Cowan (2011) states, many organizations fail to recognize bullying as harassment. Therefore, even though the behaviors and motives associated with workplace bullying are typically the same, the differences in terminology may keep people from exercising their rights, or they may not have any rights at all. Remember, human-resource departments protect the employers, not the employees. The same is true for teachers unions. Moreover, you may be hung out to dry in workplace-bullying situations, as removing a teacher is easier and less public than removing an administrator.

Teachers unions may rarely protect teachers, for the sole purpose of protecting a school district's administration and public image. Very often teachers unions and school districts are in each other's back pockets (hence the phrase *collective bargaining agreement*). A new teacher to a school district may want to avoid becoming a member of a teachers union, particularly if past cases of workplace bullying have failed to reach a positive legal conclusion for the victim. I recommend taking any money you would spend per month on teachers-union fees (thirty to forty dollars per month) and start a personal savings account instead. Use this money for legal consultations, moving fees, or other employment opportunities if such unfortunate circumstances arise.

Given that few school districts in America have anti-bullying laws or regulations on the books, a further examination of the school district's codes of conduct may ultimately protect a teacher or other school employee from such workplace-bullying behavior. Pre-service teachers and teachers who are new to a school district must acquire and keep these documents for their records. Reviewing these documents and codes of conduct rules for school employees may provide a teacher the only written proof available that a contract-breaking behavior is occurring.

RECOGNIZING WORKPLACE AGGRESSION AND BULLYING WITHIN SCHOOL ENVIRONMENTS

School staff members within an organization may not easily recognize workplace aggression or workplace bullying. Within the school environment specifically, workplace bullying can take many forms. Some manifestations are verbal, physical, and individualized. Sometimes bullying is conducted in group settings or meetings, and sometimes these episodes occur behind closed doors. Most commonly, workplace bullying and aggression can take the forms of, but are not limited to the following:

- Deliberate verbal interruption within meetings
- Face-to-face intimidation
- Lying
- Gossip or rumor spreading
- Mean or dirty looks
- Ignoring coworkers' questions publically or privately
- Making fun of coworkers' responses to questions
- Non-inclusion in social or professional meetings
- Inappropriate laughing during presentations
- Unexpected isolation during meetings
- Incomplete or poorly timed communications (via phone, e-mail or social-media)
- Passive-aggressive behaviors
- Ignoring ideas
- Unfair acknowledgment of achievements
- Unfair resource allocation
- Blatant favoritism

Dzurec, Kennison, and Albataineh (2014) state that bullying in the workplace can start with little facts being verbally shared from one person to another in an aggressive tone while the victim's sense of self is questioned, thereby leading to embarrassment, humiliation, and a sense of shame. In essence, Dzurec et al. (2014) states that shaming is a major component of intimidating coworkers into compliance or creating coworkers who are less likely to voice their opinion in the future, due to fear of retaliation or future intimidation. Dzurec et al. (2014) also describes this as *double-speak*. This phrase can be defined as a person, or group of people asking for one thing, and then when that task is accomplished, they aggressively reporting it as inaccurate or incomplete. This is also done in writing and in subtle verbal conversations between parties. This double-speak becomes a one-way conversation from the victimizer toward the victim. For example, a workplace bully may say, "I'm interested in teachers contacting parents directly to conduct parent conferences." Yet, when teachers act on that statement, that bully may use double-speak and take an aggressive tone ("Why did you contact the parent to schedule a parent conference?"). Some may also refer to this communication style as *passive-aggressive*.

Another example of double-speak involves the subtle verbal or written tones that are used within varying forms of communication between parties, or through public or private conversations (Dzurec et al., 2014). Shouting and screaming may be absent in these cases, and the verbal or written tones that are used may be calm in approach, yet the exact opposite is the intended meaning. The intent here is to inflict a control method over the individual who is deemed as the target. This approach of control through the use of subtle tones may be more common, yet it's just as harmful as shouting or screaming. If feelings such as these arise personally, or if they are witnessed within a school environment—this is workplace bullying. People exuding these aggressive behaviors are then identified as workplace bullies.

Namie and Namie (2009) state in their book titled *The Bully at Work*, that there are two categories of people regarding workplace bullying: those who are the *bullies* and those who are the *targets*.

The characteristics of bullies include the following:

- Inadequate, defensive, and poorly developed
- Paranoid
- Poor leaders, with poor social skills
- Lazy
- Possible victims of abuse earlier in life or currently

- Practitioners of favoritism
- Possible substance abusers
- "Assholes" (Sutton, 2010). From his book, *The No Asshole Rule: Building a Civilized Workplace and Surviving One That Isn't.*

The characteristics of targets include the following:

- Kind, warm, smart, and sociable
- Nice
- Hardworking
- Exceed the expectations of their contracts
- Autonomous leaders
- Ethical, honest, and possess positive attitudes

Within school environments, those subjected to workplace bullying are typically those seen as weaker, younger, and vulnerable—without full-time status or easily coercible. Elderly teachers, teacher's aids, or those who hold more secretarial positions can easily be ridiculed, manipulated, and controlled by their coworkers and superiors. Such behaviors typically occur due to the knowledge the bullies may have about the status of their target's job. If the job can be relocated or removed permanently, bullying may occur more often to receive compliance in return, as the threat of job loss can paralyze the victim.

As such interactions bring about feelings of shame or embarrassment, this is what the workplace bully is counting on. Dzurec et al. (2014) states that such bullying behaviors are never legitimate and that they always lead to long-term destructive behaviors. If such workplace bullying characteristics are supported and encouraged in the interest of demanding compliance throughout an organization or school district, this pattern of systemic malcontent is typically described as *elite deviancy.*

NEPOTISM AND WORKPLACE BULLYING

Nepotism is defined when schools or other organizations hire from within, hire their friends, hire those who graduated from that same institution in which they are currently employed, or hire and promote their family members or friends usually due to familiarity. Nepotism within school environments can be rampant. Nepotism can be falsely categorized as a hiring skill or a characteristic of organizational leadership. Neither is true. This unprofessional practice within school districts usually transpires due to the illusionary belief that when people hire based on these familiarities; leadership, compliance, and achievement will become standard practices. As it turns out, nepotism within educational organizations, depending on the state, is largely discouraged if not illegal. Nepotism gives way to complacency, corruption, laziness, unprofessionalism, and an organizational culture of workplace bullying. Nepotism can also produce a workplace culture that is reckless, and one that mimics the poisonous behaviors of a college fraternity or sorority house.

Nepotism practices also impede school-level and district-level administrators from making objective ethical decisions about whom they hire, how everyone is evaluated, and how long they retain their employees. If married couples are working in the same school, their annual evaluations are likely to be the same. If multiple generations of the same family work in the same district or within the same school, a similar outcome is expected. If one member of a relationship (personal or sexual) is responsible for evaluating his or her partner, the likelihood of that evaluation being positive is remarkably high, regardless of the factual performance levels. Some school districts have superintendents or administrators whose family members or significant others are their immediate subordinates. In essence, nepotism practices within school environments are largely deemed unfair and highly unethical.

Such practices are directly linked to workplace bullying because everyone knows of the relationship ties from one employee to the next. Regardless of the measurement tool used to evaluate the performance of school employees, the documented summary of an employee's yearly evaluation may ultimately be 100 percent subjective. Becoming the victim of such unfair practices may lead to disillusionment, dissatisfaction, and anger toward fellow coworkers or bosses.

PREVENTION MEASURES FOR WORKPLACE BULLYING WITHIN SCHOOL ENVIRONMENTS

Workplace bullying within school-based environments can occur almost anywhere and in a variety of forms. Examples of workplace bullying behaviors within school-based environments include, but are not limited to the following:

- Untimely classroom observations
- Overabundance of classroom observations
- Isolation of teachers in meetings
- Gossip about teachers and coworkers to other staff members
- Threats of job loss privately or directly
- Administrative encouragement for teachers to change student grades (typically from failing to passing.)
- Feelings of humiliation or embarrassment in front of other coworkers or students
- Unwanted physical contact
- Being yelled at, privately or publically
- Laughing at thoughts and ideas, privately or publically
- Passing off work to others that someone could easily do himself or herself
- Withholding important information
- Having unrealistic expectations for particular results (no parent conferences and no parent phone calls)
- Cheap or unfair use of rewards and recognition
- Interrupting others' conversations
- Negative comments about cloths, hair, shape, size, etc.
- E-mail, Twitter, Facebook or other online gossip about coworkers
- Attempting to one-up each other in groups
- Rewarding those hired through nepotism while devaluing others

Locations of workplace bullying within school-based environments include, but are not limited to the following:

- Faculty meetings
- Parent conferences
- Department meetings
- Hallway banter (groups of teachers standing around gossiping)
- Teacher lunchrooms/lounges
- Teacher/staff introductions in meetings

- Cafeterias
- Parent pick-up/drop-off locations
- Classrooms
- Bathrooms

Avoidance of the above locations and areas where teachers congregate may provide relief from being bullied or witnessing bullying. While many of these places are impossible to avoid, observant behavior may highlight such episodes and inform individuals of problematic behavior. The preventative measures used to monitor workplace bullying may also vary. Beyond immediate physical removal from specific situations, a written recording of each incident should be documented and kept up to date. Upon the very first infraction, the names of the individuals participating in the workplace bullying must be documented—followed by the time of day, the location, the specific behaviors witnessed, and the content spoken. Each documented occurrence must conclude with how the episodes made the victim or witnessing party feel as the event transpired.

Such documentation may take time, but it may also prove to be beneficial if counterclaims are made in an attempt to disprove one's point of view or personal recounting of an episode. If other coworkers can corroborate what you have witnessed, obtaining their opinions in writing may also be beneficial. This would add to your claims that an unhealthy work environment exists. If many coworkers witness such behaviors, continue to document each incident and describe who was in the room, and who heard or saw the behaviors being displayed.

In cases where a coworker is verbally assaulting another, there is nothing wrong with the victim standing up for him or herself. For example, "I messages" could be used in a firm tone of voice. Such messages include the following:

- I would like you to stop.
- I don't like the way you are talking to me.
- I don't like the conversation you both are having, so please stop until I leave.
- I would like you to leave, and I want you to talk to me differently next time.
- I don't appreciate your unprofessional manner.
- I need you to leave right now.

However, immediate removal from the situation by physically placing your body as far from the bully as possible may be the best option. Any retaliatory verbal exchange you provide may be used against you, or intentionally misrepresented in the future in an effort to advance a workplace bully's point of view.

There is one more serious matter that can occur within such workplaces. Sometimes an employer or organization condoning unethical practices may find out about condemning documentation that a victim or witnessing employee has been accumulating. If the organization becomes aware of documentation that exposes un-professionalism and unethical or illegal behavior, you may be bullied, lose your job, or be forced to resign for a made-up or arbitrary reason. When an actual employee who possesses this evidence exposes this documentation or evidence of wrongdoing by an organization or person within, this is defined as *whistle blowing*. Whistle blowing is defined as *an individual or individuals bringing to light the discovery of unethical, illegal, or a contract-breaking behavior regarding the rules or laws that exist within*. Whistle blowing is not illegal, and many rights can exist for whistle blowers depending on the state in which one lives.

School districts may attempt to have teachers sign gag orders in order to prevent them from telling the public about such unethical or illegal behaviors that have been discovered, witnessed, or recorded. School districts and organizations may even mon-etarily bribe a whistle blower in an effort to coerce him or her into signing a gag order. Keep in mind that gag orders are legal documents. If you sign one and you are found to break the rules or demands of a gag order, you can be sued or immediately fired. Again this is where immediate legal consultation must occur with individuals (lawyers) out-side of the organization in question. Most education lawyers would state that when an educator is presented with a gag order, he or she should never sign it. Gag orders are essentially an admission of guilt or wrong-doing on the part of the organization distributing the order. Guilty organizations always want those who have witnessed unethical behavior to stay quiet.

As it turns out, whistle blowers are typically the most ethical and morally sound individuals within a workplace (Namie & Namie, 2009). Along with their own suc-cess and the successes of others, they are typically concerned with ethical, positive, and law abiding behavior (Namie & Namie, 2009). Such behaviors should never be an unrealistic expectation within a workplace, particularly in schools, which are responsible for the well-being of children.

As stated before, legal consultation is a great preventative measure for workplace bullying. Legal expertise regarding bullying (albeit not illegal in most cases) can give teachers or other school employees the knowledge they need to report infractions to trusted parties, all while keeping the legal authorities up to date with the latest infraction. A simple Google search for *educational lawyers, workplace-bullying lawyers in my area* or *whistle-blowing law firms* can turn up a plethora of options and viable resources for immediate consultation. Just remember, most cases related to workplace bullying never make their way to court. Employees may have few if any rights, and workplace bullying is not illegal in most cases.

HEALTH EFFECTS RELATED TO WORKPLACE BULLYING

Adverse health effects can occur as a result of workplace bullying. Sansone and Sansone (2015) state that bullying in adulthood is also associated with a number of negative consequences, affecting emotional, psychological, medical, and socioeconomic areas of functioning that are not that dissimilar from childhood bullying. The negative health effects attributed to workplace bullying can include, but are not limited to the following:

- Sleep disturbances (insomnia, night sweats)
- Disinterest that may lead to disillusionment
- Anxiety
- Fatigue
- Depression
- Autoimmune conditions (hair loss, skin or joint malformations, etc.)
- Anger (public or private outbursts)
- Mood swings and other anxiety disorders
- Cardiovascular disease
- Posttraumatic stress disorder (PTSD)
- The murder of coworkers
- Workplace-related suicide

Due to the above disorders and health-related characteristics attributed to workplace bullying, psychotropic drugs and mood stabilizers can be commonly abused in response to these adverse feelings (Sansone & Sansone, 2015). In addition to these consequences of workplace bullying, there are also socioeconomic consequences. These tend to include an increase in absenteeism. Sick days can be used up, and greater rates of unemployment occur through job loss or leaving voluntarily (Sansone & Sansone, 2015). I suggest that those victims of workplace bullying and those who possess these associated health effects seek professional help from trained professionals outside of a school district. The films below are individuals describing their experiences with workplace bullying.

- https://www.youtube.com/watch?v=MQxIG4n3w5I&spfreload=10
- YouTube Search Title: *Francesco Portelos interviewed by Sharon Parella*

- https://www.youtube.com/watch?v=YmRKIZEXVQM
- YouTube Search Title: *How I survived workplace bullying | Sherry Benson-Podolchuk | TEDxWinnipeg*

Once these steps have been taken, and if no other positive measures have occurred to address or permanently remove the behaviors or the people exhibiting the workplace bullying (which most likely won't happen within a school's working environment), a teacher or school staff member should explore other employment opportunities. Most workplace bullies will never leave, nor will their organization change or hold the guilty parties accountable because of your mistreatment. I suggest going out on your own healthy terms before it's too late.

Similar to dissatisfied parents removing their child from an unsafe school, a teacher's resignation from a school district can send a powerful public message that not every school staff member will tolerate the negative behaviors being witnessed. If you resign, make your resignation professional, just, and honest, and focus on the negative treatment you endured while working there. Send your resignation to every school-district leader and administrator you worked for, along with every teacher you worked with. This way the bullying and the bullies can't hide, and the problem can be exposed publically. As Namie and Namie (2009) state, "There will always be another job. However, if a job kills you, you won't be around to work it."

SUMMARY POINTS FOR CHAPTER 10

- The core of workplace bullying is the need or attempt to harm in the interest of gaining control, typically due to feelings of inadequacy.
- Roughly half of men and half of women experience workplace bullying while employed. The same is true for those who victimize.
- College students' exposure to the knowledge of workplace bullying is remarkably low, and given their immediate interest in entering the workforce, such an education may prepare them for what may be inevitable.
- Workplace bullying has massive implications for workplace morale, personal and group health, quality of life, and the well-being of an organization's culture.
- A further examination of the school district's code of conduct may ultimately protect a teacher or other school employee from such workplace-bullying behavior.
- Workplace bullying can start with little facts being verbally shared and an aggressive tone being present. Then the victim's sense of self is questioned, thereby leading to embarrassment, humiliation, and a sense of shame.
- Shaming is a major component to intimidating one into compliance or creating a coworker who is less likely to voice his or her opinion in the future due to fear of retaliation or future intimidation.
- Getting to know numerous members of a school building can give you a workplace cultural-health perspective that may inform your future decision-making.
- Nepotism gives way to complacency, laziness, unprofessionalism, and an organization-wide culture of workplace bullying.
- Legal expertise regarding bullying (albeit not illegal in most cases) can give teachers or other school employees the knowledge they need to report infractions to trusted parties.

- Bullying in adulthood is also associated with a number of negative consequences affecting emotional, psychological, medical, and socioeconomic areas of functioning. Removing yourself from workplaces that sanction such
practices may be your best option.

11

Conflict Resolution and Violence Prevention in Education

Conflict resolution and violence prevention education can be the realistic remedy to violence among students and school staff. The information available today is easy to obtain, read, and apply if one chooses to do so. Teacher educators and school-staff members everywhere can easily examine this education and apply these proven methods.

We know that teacher education programs at the college and university level may rarely address such serious topics among their pre-service teachers. We know that current teachers in K–12 schools may not receive professional development related to the issues discussed throughout this text from supervising school administrators or other district staff members. We know that states of denial can place a chokehold on the facts. But, given the serious nature of these topics, everyone's well-being is at risk of being compromised. Everyone's achievement levels are at risk of failing to meet expectations.

A reexamination of what currently works and what has been proven to work is necessary, and their application methods should be implemented sooner rather than later. For example, the first day of school has been proven to be the most important day of the school year for children and adults. Parental communication and parental conferences can be largely discouraged or poorly managed in some schools, while positively existing in others. Peer-mentoring as a deterrent to violent behavior between students in school, may not be occurring enough, nor may it exist before a violent episode displays itself.

Along with future undergraduate training on conflict resolution, violence prevention, and the factors listed throughout this text, I would state that these methods below could also be applied with regularity. The safety and consistency of students, teachers, school administrators, and parents should be priority number one. The implementation of existing proven educational research may ultimately lead to the healthiest objective learning environments possible, which surround themselves with innovative and objective professional leaders.

THE FIRST DAY OF SCHOOL

Research on the first day of school was first introduced in the 1980s. Brooks (1985a) discovered that most teachers on the first day of school were simply interested in getting through the day and surviving. What we now know is that there are critical contexts in which lessons must be delivered and ways in which teachers must communicate with students on the first day of school (Brooks, 1985a). These contexts aim to increase engagement and decrease disciplinary action that can impact the rest of the school year (Brooks, 1985a). These methods must happen on the first day of school, every single school year.

Brooks (1985b) reported that teachers who exhibited positive behaviors through facial expressions, tone of voice, and positive manners are more successful throughout the first day of school, and this lead to further success throughout the whole school year. The inexperienced teachers, who rushed through the first day of school, used harsh tones, played games, and failed to teach the rules and behavioral expectations were more likely to struggle all year long. Teachers who were not as successful on the first day of school tended to struggle with communication and student discipline throughout the entire school year (Brooks, 1985b).

An organized sequence of instruction and positively modeling behaviors by effective teachers, also increases the chances of a successful first day of school for both the teacher and students within the classroom (professional businesslike tone of voice, friendly personality, abundant eye contact, smooth organized transitions, and a *teaching* of the rules and classroom expectations) (Brooks, 1985a). In his article titled, *The First Day of School*, Brooks (1985a) discusses what teachers should both do and not do on the first day of school. He states how these practices could either help or hurt the teacher and the students, from the first day of school forward. Brooks (1985a) reported that student's needs are very simple on the first day of school.

Student needs on the first day of school are the following:

1. Are they in the right room?
2. Where are they supposed to sit?
3. What are the rules of this teacher?
4. What will the students be doing in the course?
5. How will the students be evaluated?
6. Who is the teacher as a person?
7. Is the teacher going to be interested in them as individuals?

Brooks (1985a) states that teachers who address these student needs first and often, are likely to be more successful than those teachers who ignore the immediate needs of their students, most of which tend to be emotional.

Brooks (1985a) recommends the following sequence of activities for teachers on the first day of school:

1. Stand at the door and greet each student with a handshake and a smile, and tell them all that they can sit in any student chair they wish to sit in.
2. Call the class to order when the bell rings.
3. Take role, organize seating, and establish a seating chart at the same time.
4. Explain classroom rules and procedures.
5. Introduce the course content and grading procedures
6. Solicit student autobiographical information on three-by-five index cards.
7. Talk about yourself, your school experiences, and so forth.
8. Close with what materials will be needed the next day and what the content will cover.
9. Dismiss the class at the bell.

Most importantly, Brooks (1985a) states that the *teaching* of the rules is critical for student and teacher success. If the rules are not taught using positive and negative examples with described disciplinary action for the latter, the ambiguity of each rule will confuse students, thereby leading to increased rule breaking and classroom disorganization down the line (Brooks, 1985a).

Although this proven research has existed since the 1980s, many schools fail to address these simple needs and then later wonder why their schools are experiencing problems with conflict, violence, and disciplinary issues between teachers, administrators, and students. On the first day of school, many teachers in schools across America play "get to know you games" with students or neighboring classrooms. Other schools may have staff members pile students into auditoriums for assemblies, thereby increasing the anxiety levels among students through ambiguity. By not spending the whole day describing what is expected throughout the year within their classrooms, teachers fail to meet the immediate emotional needs of their students.

Accompanying the first day of school practices, as researched by Brooks (1985a), I would merely add one more critical strategy that also meets the emotional needs of students. **Tell your students that you care about them**. Use these exact words at the beginning and end of each class period on the first day of school ("I care about each and every one of you, and here's why."). When teachers make this statement and specifically address the importance of safety, learning, and a beneficial environment for everyone, students will be pleasantly surprised to hear this from their teacher. Most teachers may never say these words to their students on the first day of school, or any day after that throughout the course of their entire career.

After the first day of school, students will go home, and they may be asked by their families, "Who is your favorite teacher?" Or, students themselves may rush home and say, "Guess who my favorite teacher is?" As a professional educator, you want your name mentioned first to their family members. You'll want this to occur on the first day of school and every day after that. Applying the above approaches can make this a reality.

PARENT-TEACHER CONFERENCES AND PARENTAL COMMUNICATION

Parental conferences, as one might expect, can be an important tool in violence prevention and conflict resolution within school environments. In fact, it may be one of the best prevention methods and antidotes. The quality and frequency of parental conferences and parental communication is a critical step toward addressing the needs of families, the students, and the teachers.

Most parent conferences occur when something bad happens. They typically occur when a behavioral problem exists or an academic misstep has been made. These meetings can be scheduled if a teacher attempts to fix a long-standing problem or if a parent is in need of viable answers. Parental conferences occur for a variety of reasons.

Many parent conferences are also legally mandatory given students' academic accommodations regarding their ESE (exceptional student education) status or any other accommodation regarding physical, mental, behavioral, or language barrier. In every case, a teacher can learn a lot about the quality of interactions their students are having with the adults in their lives. Parents, teachers, and school staff members can expose themselves within parent conferences as being unorganized, overbearing, unprofessional, intimidating, or simply lacking compassion or honesty. Regardless of what behaviors are witnessed within parent conferences, as a teacher you can control a number of outcomes that intend to assist all parties with realistic goals and expectations.

Upon a Student's Witnessed Behavior or Academic Standing

First, parent conferences should happen often. They should occur in order to intervene in destructive habits, or even pay personal compliments regarding positive student behaviors. Kroth and Edge (2012) stated that the frequency of parental conferences could have a dramatic impact on communication among the family, the student, and the teachers. This can reduce the likelihood of future negative feedback and prevent communication problems down the line (Kroth & Edge, 2012).

Something teachers and administrators hear quite often in parent conferences is when the parents look directly at them and say, "Why didn't we hear about this sooner?" This question is a killer in a parent conference. It can expose unwillingness on the part of the school's administration and the teachers to communicate immediately with families upon recognizing a problem. Frankly, it exposes laziness. The moment there is a problem with a child's academic performance or behavior within the school, the parents should be contacted that very day and the following steps should be taken:

1. A phone call should be made to the family or guardian directly.
2. If the family contact is unavailable, leave a voice message.
3. Then follow up with an e-mail to the family contact that directly addresses the student's situation.
4. Send home a grade printout of the student's grades or assignments and hand it to the student to give to his or her parents if the issue is academic.
5. Keep a record of each type of correspondence. This way all bases are covered.

There is a long-standing belief that when such a grade form is sent home with a student, it will never see the parent's hands. At least you can say you used it as a strategy to contact the parent with all the other methods having been exhausted. If the grade sheet never reaches the parent, then the student has made a misstep that isn't your fault because of a lack of trying.

Some parents may never want, or agree to a parent conference. This is usually due to a lack of acceptance regarding the circumstances or feelings of self-shame regarding the child's behavior. In some cases, the parent may interpret that the parent conference is for them, and not really for their child. Sending a letter home that compassionately addresses any concerns may help alleviate unwillingness for the parents to meet their child's teachers in a parent conference. With signatures from all the student's teachers and a reassurance that parental input is encouraged, parents may ultimately agree to such a conference. In situations where parents refuse time and time again, the police and legal authorities may become involved in an effort to communicate consequences regarding the student's behavior or academic standing. Regardless of your positive effort, there are some things you can control and some things you can't.

Upon Notice of a Scheduled Parent Conference

When a parent conference has been scheduled, I suggest meeting with all the teachers of the student in question one day before the scheduled conference so that you can all get on the same page. Discuss the needs of the student, the student's behavior within each classroom, and the desired goals you have for the student and his or her family. Make sure you print out each grade and assignment standing for both the student and the attending family to see and take home with them. You should also include a short list of specific behaviors that may be contributing to a larger problem.

During this preliminary meeting, refrain from gossiping with other teachers about the child, the child's parents, or the child's family members. Stick to the purpose of the pre-conference meeting. Verbally redirect teachers who begin these unprofessional habits, as they can often take place. To help alleviate this unprofessional habit, pre-conference meetings and parental conferences can be organized with an *identification, diagnosis,* and *prescription* methodology. *Identify* the problem and associated parties; *diagnose* what is going on; and *prescribe* how it can be fixed. Once this is agreed upon before the parental conference, the participating teachers and staff members will now be on the same page about how to approach the situation. The last thing you want to witness in a parent-teacher conference is dissention between the staff members in front of the parents and student. This also sends the message of a lack of organization, professionalism, and leadership.

The Parent Conference

Bring every piece of written documentation you have regarding the student, and the information you want the student and parents to know before they leave the conference. Never show up empty-handed.

The only people in the room should be those who are responsible for communication with the parent. This involves the teachers of the student, the school counselor, or administrators if necessary. If the issue is a grade dispute regarding academic performance, teachers are usually the only ones involved. If the issue is behavioral, administrators and counselors should be involved. If this is the case, administrators and counselors should also attend the pre-conference meeting.

The tables and chairs within the conference space should accommodate all individuals. They should be organized in a circle pattern to highlight equality. Refrain from a head-to-head design of the tables and chairs, as to avoid an "us versus them" mentality. No one is on trial, and it's not a legal deposition. It's simply a conference to communicate and connect.

Kroth and Edge (2012) suggest applying the following steps when beginning communication with parents, particularly if the parents enter aggressively or become aggressive during the meeting:

1. Write down what parents say.
2. When they pause, ask what else is bothering them.
3. Exhaust their list of complaints.
4. Ask them to clarify any specific complaints that are too general.
5. Show them the list and ask whether it is accurate and complete.
6. Ask for their suggestions for solving any of the problems listed.
7. Write down their suggestions.
8. As much as possible, mirror their verbal and nonverbal behaviors, For example, if they speak louder, you should speak softer.

In the beginning, let the parents start with their concerns and build from there. This isn't a time to defend one another or make yourself look more competent than your coworkers. A parent conference is a time to share thoughts, share compassion, and share concern for the well-being of each party. However, this must be done with candor. As Tveit (2009) states, it's common for teachers to avoid truthfulness in the interest of being tactful. Sadly, this may prolong the problem, particularly if the issue is serious and requires immediate attention (Tveit, 2009). Truthfulness and candor are essential parts of an effective parent conference, as the sharing of unknown information between parties is essential.

Sometimes parent conferences can get sidetracked and go off the rails. They can become chatty, less focused, and drag on longer than they need to. Maintain professionalism and make sure that all parties, in the interest of moving forward, agree to the goals, objectives, and actions for the future. Keep the conference moving in a fluid and positive direction, and then conclude it in an appropriate manner.

Parental conferences can also become hostile for a number of reasons. Sometimes within parent conferences, students can become the victims, and they can be forced to tears due to an overwhelming sense that they're being ganged up on. These feelings may also come about because of a lack of understanding, empathy, or sympathy. This must be avoided at all costs. The major thing to keep in mind is that parent conferences can highlight underlying problems with the student, the family, and the teacher's relationship with that student or family. Pay close attention to how the family addresses each teacher and how the other teachers address the student.

It's very common for people to take sides in parent conferences. I recommend taking the side of justice, objectivity, common sense, and problem solving. This approach will generate a healthier student, family, and learning environment. Below are some examples of the information that can be learned in parent conferences regarding all participating parties:

- Family dynamics and divorce
- Neglect (the most common form of abuse)
- Death in the family
- Drug use
- Alcoholism within the family
- Physical or sexual abuse
- Criminal and arrest records
- Disability
- Overbearing parents
- Overbearing teachers
- Parental or family abandonment
- Unjust behavior among parents, teachers or administrators
- Inconsistent discipline or accountability practices
- Bullying in school or at home
- Unfair grading or poor practices by the teacher, counselor or administrator
- Disorganization at home or within the classroom
- Mental illness with students or other family members
- Generation gaps between family members (grandparents or older family members accepting legal guardianship)
- The need for family, group or individual professional counseling or therapy

Teachers should allow the parents to set goals in parent conferences as well. Cheatham and Ostrosky (2011) stated that too often teachers take an overbearing role in a parent conference and force goals on a student and his or her family members in the interest of demanding compliance. This can be an unhealthy approach, as parents are ultimately responsible for their child. Parents should take the lead in helping organizing goals for their child. Teachers should simply assist in this process, or make the occasional professional suggestion (Cheatham & Ostrosky, 2011). Finally, I recommend sending a follow up e-mail thanking the attending parents or family members of the student for joining the conference, and stating that you look forward to working with them again if needed.

It should be noted that this formal information about how to conduct parent conferences is typically not shared within teacher-education programs, nor is it shared once someone becomes a teacher. Too often, pre-service teachers learn about how to conduct parent conferences on the fly. Young teachers may be exposed to unprofessional practices early and often, and only after beginning the student-teaching process. This is typically too late, as some veteran teachers may not be as thorough as they need to be, or they may model unprofessional examples for younger educators. Learning more about how to conduct successful parent-teacher conferences is an essential step in the preparation and continued success of teachers and school staff.

PEER MENTORING 2.0 AND CONFLICT-RESOLUTION GROUPS

Another impactful violence-prevention approach includes peer-mentoring programs or conflict-resolution groups. This is done in an effort to connect students from other grade levels within the same school, or between different schools. Having successfully done this in the past over many years of teaching, I specifically refer to this model as peer mentoring 2.0. This is a new model of peer mentoring that operates on the preventive side of conflict and violence, instead of operating after a destructive episode.

Peer mentoring 2.0 can occur face-to-face in a classroom, or virtually using video chatting programs such as Skype. Peer-mentoring programs have gained acceptance among students over the years (Brewer & Carroll, 2010). Participation in such peer-mentoring face-to-face programs within school can increases stronger efficacy with helping others, and with taking a leadership role in such activities and within a student's own life (Brewer & Carroll, 2010). Welfare (2010) suggests that accessing the Internet in positive ways and having students connect with peers in this format can curb such methods of violence, including cyberbullying; in particular if facilitated and monitored by a vigilant professional educator. Welfare (2010) also states that while it may be difficult to keep all students off of the Internet, it's always possible to first teach them how to be safe online and utilize the technology appropriately.

Our role as teachers and effective educators, as stated by Kalin (2012), is to put students next to impactful technologies that better suit them for success now and in the future. Kalin (2012) also discussed how we as educators should teach students not only how to use the related technology for personal connection and instruction, but also how to think beyond the current moment and produce information based on a designated outcome. For example, Skype could be introduced in the classroom to enhance student learning and peer connections (Abe & Jordan, 2013).

In the design process of peer mentoring 2.0, or other conflict-resolution groups, connecting students from one grade level to another can bridge an age gap that is necessary for reflection and application (eighth grade mentors sixth grade, or twelfth grade mentors ninth grade). Within the elementary school environment, middle school students could mentor fifth-grade students on success at the middle school level and connect them to an environment that typically brings about anxious behavior upon entry. If schools and their administrators consider the needs of their environment, they might reach an agreement that the bookends of a student's education can be a great place to implement such a peer-mentoring program. The placement of this implementation at critical moments within a school year is important to consider. Suggestions for setting up peer mentoring 2.0 are below.

Organizing Peer Mentoring 2.0 Groups

1. Conduct peer mentoring at the beginning and end of the school years to allow for advice sharing, resourcing, and reflection. Students love helping other students, particularly when given the chance.
2. Mentoring can exist in every class as well. Have six to eight mentors per class.
3. Have participating mentors represent the whole-school environment (mentors should be every gender, race, background, and achievement level). Refrain from picking only straight-A students. The more mentors the mentees can relate to, the better.
4. Meet with the mentors before hand to organize the topics of discussion.

5. At the elementary level, use Skype to connect classes or schools if students cannot attend face-to-face.

6. Have permission slips filled out by mentors, parents, and teachers. Make participating school administrations aware of the activities and enlist their help if needed.

7. Encourage students to listen and ask questions, and prep your classes for the peer-mentoring session days in advance.

8. Have the mentors sit at the front of the class and take turns talking.

9. Moderate the whole discussion and keep it on point with the previously discussed topics.

10. Encourage students to reach out to the mentors anytime for help and encourage mentees to think about becoming mentors to their younger peers before they leave their current school.

Such approaches and opportunities create leaders. Brooks (2014) states that such peer-mentoring experiences allow students to form new relationships that may not have previously existed. With this process of implementation in place, peer mentoring can exist between buildings and inside a single building. During these kinds of activities, student leaders can be highlighted where they have previously been invisible, undiscovered, or underused (Brooks, 2014). Such an approach also aims to connect students who might have otherwise been divided by typical grade-level divisions. Students may never have the chance to work together or connect with one another regarding serious school-related issues. This form of peer mentoring may eradicate the old methods of grade-level division and energize new student leaders (Brooks, 2014).

In face-to-face school-based peer mentoring, positive outcomes present themselves immediately as the mentors expect to be received as competent, which creates better peer connections and overall program effectiveness (Brewer & Carroll, 2010). Mentoring can also be seen as an activity that benefits society as a whole, whose participants will engage in leadership roles and may hold decision-making positions currently, if not later in life (Brewer & Carroll, 2010). Such programs seek to improve the school's climate, and they actually do so (Brewer & Carroll, 2010). In Brewer and Carroll's (2010) study of one New York suburban high school, more student mentors held greater beliefs of self-efficacy than those who were non-mentors. Those students who had been mentors before, were more likely to become mentors again later in their educational career, as opposed to those students who had never been mentored or were never mentors themselves (Brewer & Carroll, 2010).

THE NEED FOR K–COLLEGE CONFLICT-RESOLUTION, VIOLENCE-PREVENTION, AND HEALTH EDUCATION

With educators knowing that violence is an issue in society, setting the tone for a learning environment must be shaped by the needs of the surrounding culture. As Becker, Johnson, Vail-Smith, Maahs-Fladung, Tavasso, Elmore, & Blumell (2008) report, providing college students a general health education course and related curriculum can have positive implications to their well-being throughout their early stages of adulthood. Crow (2008) states that it would be difficult to deny that such curriculum creates independent enquirers, creative thinkers, reflective learners, team workers, self-managers, and effective participators—and it could have a lasting impact on everyone's well-being. Crow (2008) also reports that schools have a responsibility to educate students for life.

Craig Zelizer of Georgetown University published an article in the *Journal of Peace Psychology* titled, *The Role of Conflict Resolution Graduate Education in Training the Next Generation of Practitioners and Scholars*. Within this article, he states that many, if not all graduate and undergraduate students are failing to receive training and education on managing diversity within their given future professions. Zelizer (2015) states that more college students and graduate students should receive a wider education beyond their major course of study in order to increase the likelihood of current and future conflict resolution. Specifically, this education involves the social sciences, psychology, political science, law, natural sciences, history, and economics. Figure 12 describes his percentage breakdown of the subjects that those within the conflict resolution field are exposed to through course work and educational experiences.

Figure 12: Disciplinary Training of the Founders of the Conflict-Resolution Field (Zelizer, 2015)

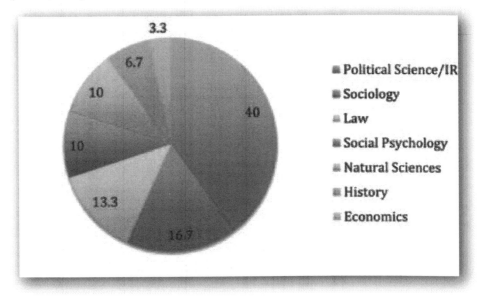

Zelizer (2015) states that a general understating of the causes of conflict and the deeper theories associated with its existence can help frame a need for resolution skills within many diverse workplace environments.

K–12, health education curriculum regarding conflict resolution and violence prevention is best highlighted within the Bronson et al. (2011) *Glencoe/McGraw-Hill Health* textbook. Within chapter 9 of the 2011 text, topics of lessons and discussions start with the following: causes of conflict; resolving conflict; understanding violence; and preventing and overcoming abuse. This chapter is placed after chapters titled "Managing Stress and Coping with Loss," "Mental and Emotional Problems," "Healthy Relationships," and "Achieving Mental and Emotional Health" (Bronson et al., 2011). The content is vocabulary rich with societal and environmental examples that allow for immediate reflection and application within students' lives. There are also online resources that put the textbook in the hands of students digitally. Becker et al. (2008) states that students who have taken such health education classes could be followed after their school experiences into adulthood, and into the workplace to measure the classes' long-term effectiveness. If access to these classes occurred at all levels of education, the implications to longer positive health outcomes would be present (Becker et al., 2008).

Lindstrom, Burke, and Gielen (2011) argue that a school's culture should place the emphasis on prevention methods to violence, not on the types of punishments they wish to administer. Discipline only exists after the problem has already occurred. Therefore, discipline approaches are not preventive methodologies for conflicts or violent behavior. Conflict resolution and violence prevention curriculum aims to educate students about conflict and violence in society and within their own culture, while preventing episodes before intervention methods are needed. Through this education, students are given the opportunity to make worldly connections that have lasting impacts beyond their current school environment.

Violence prevention and conflict resolution are just two critical components of a larger health education curriculum that should be present in today's schools, at multiple levels. This education should not be limited to K–12 schools, as college students would most certainly find this information beneficial. The case can be made that this education should exist permanently and everywhere. As Becker et al. (2008) states, all people will ultimately come to terms with their health as time goes on.

PROFESSIONALISM, CANDOR, AND LEADERSHIP IN AN ERA OF SCHOOL VIOLENCE

It's evident that pre-service education possesses a gap regarding conflict resolution and violence prevention skills for classroom teachers, administrators, and for their students. Pre-service teachers typically aren't taught about the perils of instructional aggression, neglecting student's needs, inciting violence, workplace bullying in school, competition, mental and emotional disorders, student drug use, and many other antecedents to violent behavior. Fullan (2016) states that emotional development must also be addressed, researched, and then taught as a predictor to academic achievement. Simple empathy building may not be enough, as emotional safety and human development have direct impacts on cognitive abilities (Fullan, 2016).

Given that teachers and administrators are scrutinized publically, and that social-media exposure can take a negative toll on a school's image, schoolteachers must be motivated to realistically help students in these areas of violence prevention and conflict resolution. Fullan (2016) states that teachers, and those who teach them, should focus on what behaviors they have exhibited in the past and how these very practices and behaviors may be contributing to a greater problem.

With violence existing in schools and an absence of systemic preventive instruction and health education curriculum to reduce it, it comes as no surprise that negative student and staff conversation topics can also dominate the learning environment and add to unprofessionalism (gossip, bullying, casual talk about drug use, sex, dating relationships, intellect, disabilities, etc.). Teachers and administrators have a professional responsibility to be aware of, and to intervene in all observed unprofessional conversations to shape the direction and quality of peer interactions (as stated in chapter 3) regardless of their location within a school-based environment. For example, negative conversations among students can exist and evolve without teacher or administrator intervention, even when these adults can hear the quality of the conversation. Candid intervention on these conversations is a professional necessity. With any lack of teacher or administrative intervention, these student conversations become the tolerated norm, thereby increasing the chances of conflict and violence in school. Figure 11 describes the potential impact of low teacher and administrative intervention on observed negative conversations among all parties within school environments.

Figure 13: Potential Impact of Low Teacher/Administrator Intervention on Observed Negative Conversation Topics

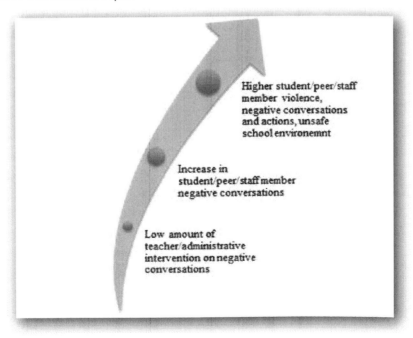

Higher student/peer/staff member violence, negative conversations and actions, unsafe school environemnt

Increase in student/peer/staff member negative conversations

Low amount of teacher/administrative intervention on negative conversations

It should be noted that any teacher or administrator at anytime—can and should immediately discourage and eliminate these unprofessional conversations or actions that may exist among students or school staff. The habit of turning a blind eye to such behaviors is easy, and sadly it's a habit that can occur with regularity. However, failure to intervene will almost certainly make a problem worse, and lead to further negative conversations or actions without proper intervention.

These conversations or actions can also exist just outside of what some may see as the teacher's boundary, such as the school bus. School buses are notorious for problematic and even deadly behavior, in particular at the conclusion of a school day. Even the periodic presence of school staff on a student populated school bus can discourage destructive behaviors among students, as these behaviors are typically beyond the sight of school officials. Teachers and administrators should never feel limited in where they can exercise their responsibility to enforce a safe environment for all students, including those locations outside of the immediate classroom. The more students trust faculty and administrators to intervene on such behaviors, the more likely they will be to report such negative incidences to their teachers, thus increasing the chances of positive intervention (O'Brennan, Waasdorp, & Bradshaw, 2014).

Intervening on negative staff and coworker conversations may be harder for an educator. Teachers and administrators within a school environment can easily have negative gossip-related conversations that are disrespectful, bigoted, and damaging to the school's culture and the individuals within. Failure to intervene in inappropriate conversations that are taking place can generate horrible short-term and long-term effects. Figure 11 above also describes these occurrences between school staff members.

Regarding negative conversations among school staff, I recommend correcting these behaviors immediately and in private. Approaching the guilty staff member or members when students are not present, is a professional way to make your feelings known about the incident. If inappropriate comments are made from school staff members toward students and other teachers are witnesses, the observing teachers should repeat the same approach as above, and they should ask for an apology on behalf of the victim. The power of an apology is an underused strategy, particularly among adults. This apology approach can send a direct message of intolerance toward any school staff that engage in hateful conversations.

Jack Welch, the former CEO of General Electric (GE), states in his book *Winning,* that "a lack of candor blocks smart ideas, fast action, and good people contributing all the stuff they've got" (p. 25). Welch (2005) states that most people within working environments don't participate in discussions of change because it's easier not to. However, a failure to intervene with candor, speed, and accuracy will most likely perpetuate any problem within any working environment. The great thing about candor is that it's viewed as an unnatural act, but it's one that is well worth it (Welch, 2005).

Welch (2005) states that leadership is not a skill that is present within everyone who holds a higher position where leadership is the expectation. There are many different kinds of leaders, and they come in many different forms. Welch (2005) states that leaders could be loud, quiet, soft, abrupt, impulsive, and analytical. Real leaders underneath are filled with warmth, compassion, kindness, and humility. They are comfortable in their own skin, and they care deeply about the growth and success of others (Welch, 2005). Young educators may have once cared about their individual success, but upon becoming educators, they must now care about the safety and success of the young lives they teach.

Welch (2005) describes eight rules of what he believes leaders do, and they are the following:

1. Leaders relentlessly upgrade their team, using every encounter as an opportunity to evaluate, coach, and build self-confidence.
2. Leaders make sure people not only see the vision but also live and breathe it.
3. Leaders get into everyone's skin, exuding positive energy and optimism.
4. Leaders establish trust with candor, transparency, and credit.
5. Leaders have the courage to make unpopular decisions and gut calls.
6. Leaders probe and push with a curiosity that borders on skepticism, making sure their questions are answered with action.
7. Leaders inspire risk taking and learning by setting the example.
8. Leaders celebrate.

The film link below is Jack Welch describing the role of a leader.

- https://www.youtube.com/watch?v=ojkOs8Gatsg
- YouTube Search Title: *What is the role of a leader?*

What continues to be evident regarding school and teacher success—is that violence prevention and conflict resolution fit within each parameter of the twenty-first-century skills for teaching and learning. Zhao (2007) states that organizations must remain competitive and ever changing within a global or local setting in order to stay relevant and increase job interest. Schoolteachers around America are leaving the profession in droves due to violent behavior among both students and school staff. A lack of acceptance regarding these problematic behaviors and a failure to intervene and better prepare pre-service teachers, current teachers, and administrators through furthering their education and professional development are most certainly contributing to the existence of the problem. Bradshaw, Waasdorp, O'Brennan, and Gulemetova (2013) state that teachers and administrators are in need of further education regarding issues related to violence, such as the ones discussed throughout this book (race, gender issues, mental and emotional disorders, frustration, suicide prevention, aggression, and bullying). I hope this book can be a tool to further this much-needed education and awareness.

Conflict resolution and violence prevention among students and school staff can be a spearhead in transforming education for the future. Each individual associated with education or schooling has a responsibility to investigate the antecedents to violent behavior. Each organization has the responsibility to bring these truthful connections to those they lead and those they teach. Effective teachers and school staff members are counting on this truth. Students and their families also count on educators and school-related organizations to reinforce professionalism, safety, learning, and happiness. Teaching and learning is a beautiful mission. Making teaching and learning healthier and safer for everyone is an achievable goal.

There's an old Cherokee Native American story that involves a conversation between a grandfather and his grandson. It's referred to as "A Tale Between Two Wolves." Here is the story:

Grandfather: There are two wolves fighting in my heart. One wolf is angry and vindictive and wishes to hurt others. The other wolf is peaceful, joyful, and loving.

Grandson: Grandfather, which wolf will win the battle of your heart?

135

Grandfather: The battle of my heart will be won by the wolf that wins the battle of every man's heart. It is the wolf I feed.

SUMMARY POINTS FOR CHAPTER 11

- An organized sequence of instruction and professional manners by the teacher also increases the chances of a successful first day of school for both the teacher and the students within the classroom.
- Teachers who address student needs on the first day of school are likely to be more successful than those teachers who ignore the immediate needs of their students, most of which tend to be emotional.
- The quality and frequency of parental conferences are a critical step in addressing the needs of the families, students, and teachers.
- Truthfulness and candor are essential parts of an effective parent conference.
- It's very common for people to take sides in parent conferences. I recommend taking the side of justice, common sense, and problem solving for a healthier student, family, and learning environment.
- Having students access the Internet to connect with peers in positive ways through teacher facilitation may curb methods of violence, including cyberbullying.
- In face-to-face school-based peer mentoring, positive outcomes present themselves immediately as presenters expect to be received as competent, which creates better peer connections and overall program effectiveness.
- Allowing mentor programs to exist with school environments seeks to improve the school climate, and they actually do so.
- More undergraduate college students and graduate students should receive a wider education beyond their majors to increase the likelihood of conflict resolution within multiple work environments. Specifically this education involves the social sciences, psychology, political science, law, natural sciences, history, and economics.
- Violence prevention and conflict resolution are just one critical component of a larger health-education curriculum that should be present in today's schools at multiple levels.

- Teachers and administrators have a responsibility to be aware of and intervene in all observed conversations to shape the direction and quality of peer interactions.

- The more students trust faculty and administrators to intervene, the more likely they will be to report such negative incidences to their teachers, thus increasing the chances of positive intervention.

- Failure to intervene if inappropriate actions are taking place can have remarkably negative short-term and long-term effects. I recommend correcting these behaviors in private where inappropriate conversations or actions exist between staff members.

- Real leaders underneath are filled with warmth, compassion, kindness, and humility.

Resources

SAFE SCHOOL ENVIRONMENTS AND SCHOOL CLIMATES

Centers for Disease Control and Prevention: Components of the Whole School, Whole Community, and Whole Child (WSCC)
https://www.cdc.gov/healthyschools/wscc/components.htm

Centers for Disease Control and Prevention: School Connectedness https://www.cdc.gov/healthyyouth/protective/school_connectedness.htm

Character.org
http://character.org/key-topics/school-climate/

Crisis Call Center
800-273-8255 or text ANSWER to 839863
Twenty-four hours a day, seven days a week
http://crisiscallcenter.org/crisisservices.html

National Center for Mental Health Promotion and Youth Violence Prevention
9:00 a.m. to 5:00 p.m. EST, Monday to Friday
http://www.promoteprevent.org

SPEAK UP

866-SPEAK-UP (773-2587)

Twenty-four hours a day, seven days a week

http://www.bradycampaign.org/our-impact/campaigns/speak-up

MENTAL AND EMOTIONAL HEALTH

Crisis Center and Hotlines Locator by State

http://www.suicidepreventionlifeline.org/getinvolved/locator

Crisis Call Center

800-273-8255 or text ANSWER to 839863

Twenty-four hours a day, seven days a week

http://crisiscallcenter.org/crisisservices.html

Depression and Bipolar Support

800-273-TALK (8255)

Twenty-four hours a day, seven days a week

http://www.dbsalliance.org

HelpGuide.org

http://www.helpguide.org/articles/emotional-health/improving-emotional-health.htm

Mental Health America (MHA)

http://www.mentalhealthamerica.net/healthy-mental-and-emotional-development

National Hopeline Network

800-SUICIDE (784-2433)

800-442-HOPE (4673)

Twenty-four hours a day, seven days a week

http://www.hopeline.com

SUICIDE PREVENTION

ImAlive: An Online Crisis Network

https://www.imalive.org

National Suicide Prevention Lifeline

1-800-273-8255

Twenty-four hours a day, seven days a week

http://www.suicidepreventionlifeline.org

Twitter: https://twitter.com/800273TALK

State Suicide Hotlines

http://www.suicide.org/suicide-hotlines.html

Suicide Prevention Services Depression Hotline

630-482-9696

Twenty-four hours a day, seven days a week

http://www.spsamerica.org

Thursday's Child National Youth Advocacy Hotline

800-USA-KIDS (800-872-5437)

Twenty-four hours a day, seven days a week

http://www.thursdayschild.org

Your Life Iowa: Bullying Support and Suicide Prevention

(855) 581-8111 (24/7) or text TALK to 85511 (4:00 p.m. to 8:00 p.m. every day)

Chat is available Mondays through Thursdays from 7:30 p.m. to midnight

http://www.yourlifeiowa.org

ALCOHOL AND DRUG PREVENTION

Al-Anon/Alateen

888-425-2666

8:00 a.m. to 6:00 p.m. EST, Monday to Friday

http://www.al-anon.alateen.org/index.php

The National Alcohol and Substance Abuse Information Center
800-784-6776
Twenty-four hours a day, seven days a week
http://www.addictioncareoptions.com

National Institute on Alcohol Abuse and Alcoholism
800-662-HELP (4357)
Twenty-four hours a day, seven days a week
http://www.niaaa.nih.gov

BULLYING AND CYBERBULLYING

American Psychological Association
http://www.apa.org/topics/bullying/

BeyondBlue
https://www.youthbeyondblue.com/understand-what's-going-on/bullying-and-cyberbullying

Centers for Disease Control and Prevention: Search *Bullying*
http://www.cdc.gov/features/prevent-bullying/
http://www.cdc.gov/ncbddd/disabilityandsafety/bullying.html

Crisis Call Center
800-273-8255 or text ANSWER to 839863
Twenty-four hours a day, seven days a week
http://crisiscallcenter.org/crisisservices.html

Cybertipline
800-843-5678
Twenty-four hours a day, seven days a week
http://www.cybertipline.com

SEXUAL HARASSMENT AND SEXUAL/PHYSICAL VIOLENCE

American Sexual Health Association
919-361-8488
8:00 a.m. to 8:00 p.m. EST, Monday to Friday
http://www.ashastd.org

Centers for Disease Control (CDC) INFO
800-CDC-INFO (232-4636)
Twenty-four hours a day, seven days a week
http://www.cdc.gov

Crisis Call Center
800-273-8255 or text ANSWER to 839863
Twenty-four hours a day, seven days a week
http://crisiscallcenter.org/crisisservices.html

GLBT National Youth Talkline
800-246-PRIDE (7743)
4:00 p.m. to midnight EST, Monday to Friday
Noon to 5:00 p.m. EST, Saturday
http://www.glnh.org/talkline

National Teen Dating Abuse Helpline
(866) 331-9474
Twenty-four hours a day, seven days a week
http://www.loveisrespect.org

National Domestic Violence Hotline
800-799-SAFE (7233)
Twenty-four hours a day, seven days a week
http://www.ndvh.org

Rape, Abuse, and Incest National Network
800-656-HOPE (4673)
Twenty-four hours a day, seven days a week
http://www.rainn.org

Safe Horizon's Rape, Sexual Assault, and Incest Hotline
Domestic Violence Hotline: 800-621-HOPE (4673)
Crime Victims Hotline: 866-689-HELP (4357)
Rape, Sexual Assault, and Incest Hotline: 212-227-3000
TDD phone number for all hotlines: 866-604-5350
Twenty-four hours a day, seven days a week
http://www.safehorizon.org

WORKPLACE BULLYING
Workplace Bullying Institute
http://www.workplacebullying.org

Workplace Bullying Institute For Teachers
http://www.workplacebullying.org/tag/teachers/

Workplace Bullying Institute YouTube Channel https://www.youtube.com/user/
BullyingInstitute?spfreload=10

CONFLICT RESOLUTION AND VIOLENCE PREVENTION IN EDUCATION
McGraw-Hill Education: Health, Fitness, and Wellness
http://www.mheducation.com/preK–12/category.30720.html

ASCD: Association for Supervision and Curriculum Development
http://www.ascd.org/about-ascd.aspx

Centers for Disease Control and Prevention—Injury Prevention and Control: Division of Violence Prevention
http://www.cdc.gov/violenceprevention/youthviolence/schoolviolence/prevention.
html

Good Character.com

http://www.goodcharacter.com/BCBC/PreventingConflicts.html

Just Say Yes: Youth Equipped to Succeed

https://www.justsayyes.org/mentors-peer-to-peer/

Journal of School Violence

http://www.tandfonline.com/loi/wjsv20?selectedTab=citation&emc=nv#.
V5-xamUdtw8

Journal of School Health—American School Health Association

http://www.ashaweb.org/resources/journal-of-school-health/

The Peace Center: Project Peace

http://www.thepeacecenter.org/programs/project-peace-for-schools/

References

Abbott, C. H., & Zakriski, A. L. (2014). Grief and attitudes toward suicide in peers affected by a cluster of suicides as adolescents. *Suicide & Life-Threatening Behavior, 44*(6), 668–681. doi:10.1111/sltb.12100

Abe, P., & Jordan, N. A. (2013). Integrating social media into the classroom curriculum. *About Campus, 18*(1), 16–20.

Agnew, R. (2001). Building on the foundation of general strain theory: Specifying the types of strain most likely to lead to crime and delinquency. *Journal of Research in Crime and Delinquency, 38*(4), 319–361. doi:10.1177/0022427801038004001

Agnew, R. (2005). *Pressured into crime: An overview of general strain theory.* Los Angeles: Roxbury.

Alvarez McHatton, P., Farmer, J. L., Bessette, H. J., Shaunessy-Dedrick, E., & Ray, S. E. (2014). Investigating middle school students' perceptions of their learning environments through drawings. *Middle Grades Research Journal, 9*(2), 37–56.

American Psychiatric Association. (2013). *Diagnostic and statistical manual of mental disorders* (5th ed.). Washington, DC: Author.

Anderman, E. M., and Murdock, T. (2007). *Psychology of academic cheating.* San Diego: Elsevier.

Anderson, E. (2012). Inclusive masculinity in a physical education setting. *Thymos: Journal of Boyhood Studies, 6*(1/2), 151–165.

Atkinson, M., & Kehler, M. (2012). Boys bullying and bio-pedagogies in physical education. *Thymos: Journal of Boyhood Studies, 6*(1/2), 166–185.

Bala, K. (2014). Social media and changing communication patterns. *Global Media Journal: Indian Edition, 5*(1), 1–6.

Bandura, A. (2016). *Moral disengagement: How people do harm and live with themselves.* New York: Worth Publishers.

Becker, C. M., Johnson, H., Vail-Smith, K., Maahs-Fladung, C., Tavasso, D., Elmore, B., & Blumell, C. (2008). Making health happen on campus: A review of a required general education health course. *Journal of General Education, 57*(2), 67–74.

Bejerot, S., Edgar, J., & Humble, M. (2011). Poor performance in physical education—a risk factor for bully victimization. A case-control study. *Acta Paediatrica, 100*(3), 413–419. doi:10.1111/j.1651-2227.2010.02016.x

Blair, R. J. (2010). Psychopathy, frustration, and reactive aggression: the role of ventromedial prefrontal cortex. *British Journal of Psychology, 101*(3), 383–399. doi:10.1348/000712609X418480

Booth, B., Van Hasselt, V. B., and Vecchi, G. M. (2011). Addressing school violence. *FBI Law Enforcement Bulletin.* Retrieved from https://leb.fbi.gov/2011/may/addressing-school-violence

Bradshaw, C. P., Waasdorp, T. E., O'Brennan, L. M., & Gulemetova, M. (2013). Teachers' and education support professionals' perspectives on bullying and prevention: Findings from a national education association study. *School Psychology Review, 42*(3), 280.

Brener, N. D., Wechsler, H., & McManus, T. (2013). How school healthy is your state? A state-by-state comparison of school health practices related to a healthy school environment and health education. *Journal of School Health, 83*(10), 743–749 doi:10.1111/josh.12089

Brewer, C., & Carroll, J. (2010). Half of the equation: Social interest and self-efficacy levels among high school volunteer peer mentors vs. their non-mentor peers. *Journal of School Counseling,* 81–27.

Bronson, M. H., Cleary, J. M., & Hubbard, B. M. (2011). *Glencoe Health.* Woodland Hills, CA: Glencoe/McGraw-Hill.

Brooks, D. M. (1985a). The first day of school. *Educational Leadership, 42*(8), 76–78.

Brooks, D. M. (1985b). The teacher's communicative competence: The first day of school. *Theory into Practice, 24*(1), 63.

Brooks, S. M. (2014). Student voices against bullying. *American Middle Level Education Association Magazine, 1*(8).

Cardon, P. W., & Marshall, B. (2015). The hype and reality of social media use for work collaboration and team communication. *Journal of Business Communication, 52*(3), 273–293. doi:10.1177/2329488414525446

Cassady, J. C., & Cross, T. L. (2006). A factorial representation of suicidal ideation among academically gifted adolescents. *Journal for the Education of the Gifted, 29*(3), 290–304.

Centers for Disease Control and Prevention. (2013). *Mental health surveillance among children—United States 2005–2011.* MMWR 2013;62 (May 16, 2013):1-35.

Centers for Disease Control and Prevention. (2013). *Trends in the prevalence of marijuana, cocaine, and other illegal drug use national YRBS: 1991—2013*. Retrieved from http://www.cdc.gov/healthyyouth/data/yrbs/index.htm

Centers for Disease Control and Prevention. (2015). *Division of Violence Prevention*. Retrieved from http://www.cdc.gov/violenceprevention/pub/youth_suicide.html

Center for the Prevention of School Violence. (2002). *Just what is "school violence"*? Retrieved from http://www.ncdjjdp.org/cpsv/pdf_ files/newsbrief5_02.pdf

Chang, B., Chuang, M., & Ho, S. (2013). Understanding students' competition preference in multiple-mice supported classroom. *Journal of Educational Technology & Society, 16*(1), 171–182.

Charmaraman, L., Jones, A. E., Stein, N., & Espelage, D. L. (2013). Is it bullying or sexual harassment? Knowledge, attitudes, and professional development experiences of middle school staff. *Journal of School Health, 83*(6), 438–444. doi:10.1111/josh.1204

Cheatham, G. A., & Ostrosky, M. M. (2011). Whose expertise?: An analysis of advice giving in early childhood parent-teacher conferences. *Journal of Research in Childhood Education, 25*(1), 24–44.

Clark, Michael D. (2016, April 23). Daylight Prom a magical event in Butler, Warren counties. *The Journal News*, pp. A1, B8.

Cowan, R. L. (2011). "Yes, we have an anti-bullying policy, but...": HR professionals' understandings and experiences with workplace bullying policy. *Communication Studies, 62*(3), 307–327. doi:10.1080/10510974.2011.553763

Crow, F. (2008). Learning for well-being: Personal, social and health education and a changing curriculum. *Pastoral Care in Education, 26*(1), 43–51.

Dewey, J. (1938). *Experience and education*. New York: MacMillan.

Dinkes, R., Cataldi, E. F., Lin-Kelly, W., and Snyder, T. D. (2007). *Indicators of school crime and safety*. Washington, DC: US Department of Education, National Center for Education Statistics.

Duan, L., Chou, C., Andreeva, V., & Pentz, M. (2009). Trajectories of peer social influences as long-term predictors of drug use from early through late adolescence. *Journal of Youth & Adolescence, 38*(3), 454–465. doi:10.1007/s10964-008-9310-y

Dzurec, L. C., Kennison, M., & Albataineh, R. (2014). Unacknowledged threats proffered "in a manner of speaking": Recognizing workplace bullying as shaming. *Journal of Nursing Scholarship, 46*(4), 281–291 11p. doi:10.1111/jnu.12080

Eom, E., Restaino, S., Perkins, A. M., Neveln, N., & Harrington, J. W. (2015). Sexual harassment in middle and high school children and effects on physical and mental health. *Clinical Pediatrics, 54*(5), 430–438. doi:10.1177/0009922814553430

Espelage, D., Anderman, E. M., Brown, V. E., Jones, A., Lane, K. L., McMahon, S. D., Reynolds, C. R. (2013). Understanding and preventing violence directed against teachers: Recommendations for a national research, practice, and policy agenda. *American Psychologist, 68*(2), 75–87. doi:10.1037/a0031307

Espelage, D. L., Low, S. K., & Jimerson, S. R. (2014). Understanding school climate, aggression, peer victimization, and bully perpetration: Contemporary science, practice, and policy. *School Psychology Quarterly, 29*(3), 233–237. doi:10.1037/spq0000090

Ferguson, C. J., Muñoz, M. E., Garza, A., & Galindo, M. (2014). Concurrent and prospective analyses of peer, television and social media influences on body dissatisfaction, eating disorder symptoms and life satisfaction in adolescent girls. *Journal of Youth & Adolescence, 43*(1), 1–14. doi:10.1007/s10964-012-9898-9

Finn, K. V. (2012). Marijuana use at school and achievement-linked behaviors. *High School Journal*, 95(3), 3–13.

Fives, C., Kong, G., Fuller, J., & DiGiuseppe, R. (2011). Anger, aggression, and irrational beliefs in adolescents. *Cognitive Therapy & Research*, 35(3), 199–208. doi:10.1007/s10608-009-9293-3

Fullan, M. (2016). *The new meaning of educational change* (5th ed.). New York: Teachers College Press.

Gome-Garibello, C., Sayka, C., Moore, K., & Talwar, V. (2013). Educators' ability to detect true and false bullying statements. *Educational Research Quarterly*, 37(1), 3–23.

Griffin, M. M., & Lake, R. L. (2012). Social networking postings: Views from school principals. *Education Policy Analysis Archives*, 20(11).

Hall, R., & Lewis, S. (2014). Managing workplace bullying and social media policy: Implications for employee engagement. *Academy of Business Research Journal*, 1, 128–138.

Hamer den, A., Konijn, E. A., & Keijer, M. G. (2014). Cyberbullying behavior and adolescents' use of media with antisocial content: a cyclic process model. *Cyber psychology, Behavior and Social Networking*, 17(2), 74–81. doi:10.1089/cyber.2012.0307

Henry, K. (2010). Academic achievement and adolescent drug use: an examination of reciprocal effects and correlated growth trajectories. *Journal of School Health*, 80(1), 38–43. doi:10.1111/j.1746-1561.2009.00455.x

Hill, A. (2008, August 31). Depression, stressed: Teachers in crisis. *The Guardian*. Retrieved from http://www.theguardian.com/education/2008/aug/31/teaching.teachersworkload

Hinduja, S., & Patchin, J. W. (2010). Bullying, cyberbullying, and suicide. *Archives of Suicide Research, 14*(3), 206–221. doi:10.1080/13811118.2010.494133

Hoffer, E. (1951). *The true believer: Thoughts on the nature of mass movements* (1st ed.). New York: Harper and Row.

Jamal, F., Fletcher, A., Harden, A., Wells, H., Thomas, J., & Bonell, C. (2013). The school environment and student health: a systematic review and meta-ethnography of qualitative research. *BMC Public Health, 13*(1), 1–11. doi:10.1186/1471-2458-13-798

Jameson, D. (2007). Competition in the classroom. *Business Communication Quarterly, 70*(2), 212–216.

Jan, A., & Husain, S. (2015). Bullying in Elementary Schools: Its Causes and Effects on Students. *Journal of Education and Practice, 6*(19), 43–56.

Joiner, S. E., Hall, R. R., & Richardson, R. E. (2015). An analysis of college students' perceptions of workplace bullying. *Academy of Business Research Journal,* 419–31.

Kajs, L. T., Schumacher, G., & Vital, C. A. (2014). Physical assault of school personnel. *Clearing House, 87*(3), 91–96. doi:10.1080/00098655.2014.891879

Kalin, J. (2012). Doing what comes naturally? Student perceptions and use of collaborative technologies. *International Journal for the Scholarship of Teaching & Learning, 6*(1), 1.

King, K. A., & Vidourek, R. A. (2012). Teen depression and suicide: Effective prevention and intervention strategies. *Prevention Researcher, 19*(4), 15–17.

Kitchen, J., & Bellini, C. (2012). Addressing lesbian, gay, bisexual, transgender, and queer (LGBTQ) issues in teacher education: Teacher candidates' perceptions. *Alberta Journal of Educational Research, 58*(3), 444–460.

Kolbert, J. B., Crothers, L. M., Bundick, M. J., Wells, D. S., Buzgon, J., Berbary, C.,...Senko, K. (2015). Teachers' perceptions of bullying of lesbian, gay, bisexual, transgender, and questioning (LGBTQ) students in a southwestern Pennsylvania sample. *Behavioral Sciences, 5*(2), 247–263. doi:10.3390/bs5020247

Kreager, D. A. (2007). Unnecessary roughness? School sports, peer networks, and male adolescent violence. *American Sociological Review, 72*(5), 705–724.

Kroth, R. L., & Edge, D. (2012). Parent conferences for school counselors and teachers. *Counseling & Human Development, 44*(9), 1–8.

Leisner, P. (1988, February 12). Students' lunchroom shooting rampage injures three educators. *Associated Press.* Retrieved from http://www.apnewsarchive.com/1988/Student-s-Lunchroom-Shooting-Rampage-Injures-Three-Educators/id-490d284859811cc6ae52f31a46fb3141

Lichty, L., Torres, J., Valenti, M., & Buchanan, N. (2008). Sexual harassment policies in K–12 schools: Examining accessibility to students and content. *Journal of School Health, 78*(11), 607–614. doi:10.1111/j.1746-1561.2008.00353.x

Lindstrom J. S., Burke, J. G., & Gielen, A. C. (2011). Prioritizing the school environment in school violence prevention efforts. *Journal of School Health, 81*(6), 331–340.

Lormand, D. K., Markham, C. M., Peskin, M. F., Byrd, T. L., Addy, R. C., Baumler, E., & Tortolero, S. R. (2013). Dating violence among urban, minority, middle school youth and associated sexual risk behaviors and substance use. *Journal of School Health, 83*(6), 415–421.

McDougall, T. (2010). Fostering resilience in children and young people. *British Journal of Wellbeing,1*(4), 35–43.

McDougall, T. (2011). Mental health problems in childhood and adolescence. *Nursing Standard, 26*(14), 48–56.

Mcintosh, J., Macdonald, F., & Mckeganey, N. (2003). The initial use of drugs in a sample of pre-teenage schoolchildren: The role of choice, pressure and influence. *Drugs: Education, Prevention & Policy, 10*(2), 147. doi:10.1080/0968763021000061092

Milgram, S. (1992). *The individual in a social world: Essays and experiments.* New York: Addison-Wesley Publishing Company.

Mueller, A. S., James, W., Abrutyn, S., & Levin, M. L. (2015). Suicide ideation and bullying among US adolescents: Examining the intersections of sexual orientation, gender, and race/ethnicity. *American Journal of Public Health, 105*(5), 980–985. doi:10.2105/AJPH.2014.302391

Nahapetyan, L. Orpinas, P., Song, X., & Holland, K. (2014). Longitudinal association of suicidal ideation and physical dating violence among high school students. *Journal of Youth & Adolescence, 43*(4), 629–640. doi:10.1007/s10964-013-0006-6

Namie, G. & Namie, R. (2009). *The bully at work: What you can do to stop the hurt and reclaim your dignity on the job.* Naperville, IL: Sourcebooks, INC.

The National Institute on Drug Abuse. (2010). *NIDA infofacts: High school and youth trends.* Retrieved from http://drugabuse.gov/infofacts/hsyouthtrends.html

The National Institute of Mental Health. (1985).Mood disorders: pharmacologic prevention of recurrences. *Am J Psychiatry, 142*(4), 469–476.

The National Institute of Mental Health. (2015). Retrieved from http://www.nimh.nih.gov/health/publications/anxiety-disorders-in-children-and-adolescents/index.shtm.

Noonan, J. H., & Vavra, M. C. (2007). *Crimes in schools and colleges: A study of offenders and arrestees reported via national incident-based reporting system data.* Federal Bureau of Investigation: Washington, DC.

North Carolina Department of Juvenile Justice and Delinquency Prevention—Center for the Prevention of School Violence. (2002). *Report on Department of Juvenile Justice and Delinquency Prevention—Center for the Prevention of School Violence's alternative to short-term suspension research.* Retrieved from http://test.ncdjjdp. org/cpsv/pdf_files/S71_Final.PDF

O'Brennan, L. M., Waasdorp, T. E., & Bradshaw, C. P. (2014). Strengthening bullying prevention through school staff connectedness. *Journal of Educational Psychology, 106*(3), 870–880. doi:10.1037/a0035957

Orlando, A. (2012, December 17). Man from 1988 Pinellas Park High School shooting: "There are no preventable measures." *Tampa Bay Times.* Retrieved from http://www.tampabay.com/news/publicsafety/man-from-1988-pinellas-park-high-school-shooting-there-are-no-preventable/1266574.

Orosz, G., Farkas, D., & Roland-Lévy, C. (2013). Are competition and extrinsic motivation reliable predictors of academic cheating? *Frontiers in Psychology, 4.* doi:10.3389/fpsyg.2013.00087

Orpinas, P., Horne, A. M., Song, X., Reeves, P. M., & Hsieh, H. (2013). Dating trajectories from middle to high school: Association with academic performance and drug use. *Journal of Research on Adolescence, 23*(4), 772–784. doi:10.1111/jora.12029

Pas, E. T., Bradshaw, C. P., Hershfeldt, P. A., & Leaf, P. J. (2010). A multilevel exploration of the influence of teacher efficacy and burnout on response to student problem behavior and school-based service Use. *School Psychology Quarterly, 25*(1), 13–27. doi:10.1037/a0018576

Perkins, H. W., Perkins, J. M., & Craig, D. W. (2014). No safe haven: Locations of harassment and bullying victimization in middle schools. *Journal of School Health, 84*(12), 810–818. doi:10.1111/josh.12208

Pew Research Center. (2015). *Social media usage: 2005–2015.* Retrieved from http://www.pewinternet.org/2015/10/08/social-networking-usage-2005-2015/

Pratt, L. A., & Brody, D. J. (2008). Depression in the United States household population, 2005–2006. *NCHS Data Brief, 7*, 1–8.

Rice, E., Petering, R., Rhoades, H., Winetrobe, H., Goldbach, J., Plant, A.,...Kordic, T. (2015). Cyberbullying perpetration and victimization among middle-school students. *American Journal of Public Health, 105*(3), 66–72. doi:10.2105/AJPH.2014.302393

Richard, J. F., Schneider, B. H., & Mallet, P. (2012). Revisiting the whole-school approach to bullying: Really looking at the whole school. *School Psychology International, 33*(3), 263–284.

Root, T., & McKay, S. (2014). Student awareness of the use of social media screening by prospective employers. *Journal of Education for Business, 89*(4), 202–206. doi:10.1 080/08832323.2013.848832

Sansone, R. A., & Sansone, L. A. (2015). Workplace bullying: A tale of adverse consequences. *Innovations in Clinical Neuroscience, 12*(1/2), 32–37.

Schad, M., Szwedo, D., Antonishak, J., Hare, A., & Allen, J. (2008). The broader context of relational aggression in adolescent romantic relationships: Predictions from peer pressure and links to psychosocial functioning. *Journal of Youth & Adolescence, 37*(3), 346–358. doi:10.1007/s10964-007-9226-y

Shields, E. J. (1999). Intimidation and violence by males in high school athletics. *Adolescence, 34*(135), 503–521.

Singh, R. D., Jimerson, S. R., Renshaw, T., Saeki, E., Hart, S. R., Earhart, J., & Stewart, K. (2011). A summary and synthesis of contemporary empirical evidence regarding the effects of the Drug Abuse Resistance Education Program (DARE). *Contemporary School Psychology, 15*, 93–102.

Steinfeldt, J. A., Vaughan, E. L., LaFollette, J. R., & Steinfeldt, M. C. (2012). Bullying among adolescent football players: Role of masculinity and moral atmosphere. *Psychology of Men & Masculinity, 13*(4), 340–353. doi:10.1037/a0026645

Sutton, R. I. (2010). *The no asshole rule: Building a civilized workplace and surviving one that isn't.* New York: Business Plus.

Taliaferro, L., Rienzo, B., & Donovan, K. (2010). Relationships between youth sport participation and selected health risk behaviors from 1999 to 2007. *Journal of School Health, 80*(8), 399–410. doi:10.1111/j.1746-1561.2010.00520.x

Tupper, K. W. (2014). Sex, drugs and the honor roll: The perennial challenges of addressing moral purity issues in schools. *Critical Public Health, 24*(2), 115–131. doi:10.1080/09581596.2013.86251

Tveit, A. D. (2009). Conflict between truthfulness and tact in parent-teacher conferences. *Scandinavian Journal of Disability Research, 11*(4), 237–256. doi:10.1080/15017410902831346

Vega, G., & Comer, D. R. (2005). Sticks and stones may break your bones, but words can break your spirit: Bullying in the workplace. *Journal of Business Ethics, 58,* 101–109. doi:10.1007/s10551-005- 1422-7

Veliz, P., & Shakib, S. (2012). Interscholastic sports participation and school-based delinquency: Does participation in sport foster a positive high school environment? *Sociological Spectrum, 32*(6), 558–580. doi:10.1080/02732173.2012.700837

Welch, J., & Welch, S. (2005). *Winning.* New York: Harper Business Publishers.

Welfare, J. (2010). Combating cyberbullying through peer mentoring. *British Journal of School Nursing, 5*(6), 296–297.

Whaley, R. B., Smith, J. M., & Hayes-Smith, R. (2011). Teenage drug and alcohol use: Comparing individual and contextual effects. *Deviant Behavior, 32*(9), 818–845. doi:10.1080/01639625.2010.538351

White, N., La Salle, T., Ashby, J. S., & Meyers, J. (2014). A brief measure of adolescent perceptions of school climate. *School Psychology Quarterly, 29*(3), 349–359. doi:10.1037/spq0000075

Wiederhold, B. K. (2014). Cyberbullying and LGBTQ youth: a deadly combination. *Cyber psychology, Behavior and Social Networking, 17*(9), 569–570. doi:10.1089/cyber.2014.1521

Wilkins, A. (2012). Push and pull in the classroom: Competition, gender and the neo-liberal subject. *Gender and Education, 24*(7), 765–781.

Winchester, D. (2008, February 11). Sad day to pass unnoticed. *Tampa Bay Times.* Retrieved from http://www.sptimes.com/2008/02/11/Southpinellas/Sad_day_to_pass_unnot.shtml

World Health Organization. (2001). *Strengthening mental health promotion* (Fact Sheet No. 220). Geneva: World Health Organization.

Yang, J., Peek-Asa, C., Corlette, J., Cheng, G., Foster, D., & Albright, J. (2007). Prevalence of and risk factors associated with symptoms of depression in competitive collegiate student athletes. *Clin J Sport Med, 17*(6), 481–487. doi:10.1097/JSM.0b013e31815aed6b

Zelizer, C. (2015). The role of conflict resolution graduate education in training the next generation of practitioners and scholars. *Peace and Conflict: Journal of Peace Psychology, 21*(4), 589–603. doi:10.1037/pac0000135

Zhao, Y. (2007). Education in the flat world: Implications of globalization on education. *EDge, 2*(4), 1–19. Retrieved from http://zhaolearning.com/wp-content/uploads/2011/02/KappanEdgeZhao.pdf

Acknowledgments

I'd like to thank those individuals who were instrumental in the creation of this book. I'd like to thank Dr. Mark Pearcy for his foreword and review of the manuscript. Thank you to Partners in Learning for their support of this manuscript and their dedication to teacher education. Thank you to Holli Bryan for her editorial work of the manuscript and to Chris Berge for his cover design. To Emilie Olsen and the Olsen family. May everyone understand the loss, prevent it from ever happening again, and may we always believe in accountability. Finally to my family, thank you.

About the Author

Dr. Sean M. Brooks earned his B.S. in Health Education from Miami University. He earned an M.S. in Education with a specialization in technology integration in the classroom and a Ph.D. in Education with a specialization in learning, instruction and innovation from the Richard W. Riley College of Education and Leadership at Walden University.

For nine years, Dr. Brooks taught math, science, health education, anatomy and physiology at the public school level, grades six through twelve. Dr. Brooks pioneered Peer Mentoring 2.0 and conflict resolution groups which included middle school, high school, and college students mentoring one another both face-to-face and using Skype in the classroom. Dr. Brooks also worked as an adjunct professor of education and student-teaching supervisor at Miami University.

Dr. Brooks has spoken at national education conferences and lectured at the university level on the topics of conflict resolution and violence prevention in school, teacher education, teacher leadership, curriculum and instruction, classroom management, and health-education advocacy.

Made in the USA
Middletown, DE
28 April 2018